ORAL TRADITIONS
FROM THE AFRICAN DIASPORA

ORAL TRADITIONS FROM THE AFRICAN DIASPORA

PETRA VOGLER

Bibliographical Information of the Deutsche Nationalbibliothek

This publication is listed in the Deutsche Nationalbibliographie of the

Deutsche Nationalbibliothek; detailed bibliographical information

can be accessed under http: //dnb.d-nb.de

Painting Cover: El Soñador by Petra Vogler, 2005

Printed and published by: BoD - Books on Demand, Norderstedt

ISBN: 9 78-3-7543-0555-3

CONTENT

INTRODUCTION

In the book 'Oral Traditions from the African Diaspora' the author reflects upon existing knowledge traditions embedded in the cultural systems of two major islands of the Atlantic Ocean, namely Cuba and Cape Verde. The traditions portrayed encompass stories, myths, legends, rituals, songs, prayers and oracle systems touching upon existing belief, religious and spiritual systems. The articles are organized in chronological order as per the research agenda, so starting with the first one on Cape Verde (2018) and the second and third one on Cuba (2019 and 2021).

The first article 'Modern Myths, Oral Narratives of the Cape Verdean Archipelago' deals with examples of famous Cape-Verdean' modern (majorly) oral narrative manifested in the form of myths such as the story about the ox Blimundo. The narration of myths/estórias – in Cape Verdean Creole (crioulo) -, can be seen as a way to accompany processes of individuation and identification as well as a means to support identity-creation and -stabilization.

The second and the third articles are based on research into two major Cuban ethnic groups, namely la lucumí or yoruba (lucumi being the liturgical language of the Santería tradition) of West African origin and la conga or the bantu of Central African origin. Accordingly, two large belief or spiritual systems can be differentiated: La Santería/Regla de Ochá, also called La Regla de Ifá or Lucumí (Yoruba), and Palo Monte/Las Reglas de Congo, also called La Regla de Mayombe (Bantu), in short regla lucumí and regla conga (cf. Cabrera 1993: 70). The second essay 'Pataki (Patakines) and Divination Systems in Cuba and their foundation in the Ifá Oracle' looks into the oral tradition of sharing myths in form of stories and the predominant divination systems of the island. The third essay 'Death and Migration in the Cuban tradition of Palo Monte Mayombe' elaborates on the central beliefs circulating around the veneration of spirits and natural earth powers.

I

MODERN MYTHS – ORAL NARRATIVES OF THE CAPE VERDEAN ARCHIPELAGO

Abstract

The interpenetration of the two major cultural groups that formed the basic societal structures of the Cape Verdean islands, the "Europeans (above all the Portuguese)" and the "West-Africans" in their roles as colonizers and colonized, disembogued into the development of a Cape Verdean culture (o caboverdiano) and into a process of creolization (crioulização). Although apparently in today's society a harmonic form of ethnic living-together seems to be installed in Cape Verdean everyday life, ambivalence with regards to perceiving and acknowledging African and European roots and influences still prevails in many aspects of individual and social existence. As important still oral cultural practice, the narration of myths/estórias – mostly in Cape Verdean Creole (crioulo) -, can be seen as a way to accompany processes of individuation and identification as well as a means to support identity-creation and -stabilization.

Keeping in mind that Atlantic slavery was abolished selectively in 1857 and in totality in 1878[1], the long history of inequality has left its traces and led nowadays

---

1   "(...), set within a longer period that began with international conventions prohibiting slave trafficking north of the equator and ended with the imperfect end of Atlantic slavery in the 1880s. Several dynamic

to a vivid reflection process of this personally embodied ambivalence as well as to a strong search for subjective individuation and identification. Further more the Cape Verdean archipelago is also an area that has always been shattered by "a dynamic admixture of phenomena – ecological crisis, epidemic disease, the advent of South Atlantic steamship service, experimentations in free soil, and imperial renewal – (Williams, D. 2015: 160)."

As a pedagogical system the myths/estórias – such as "Ti Lobo" and "Blimundo" – can help Cape Verdeans to better understand the opposing sides and contrasts of social and personal life, to integrate their European and African past and to cope with everyday situations and big problems the archipelago was facing in the past and is still facing today.

1.   Localization of the Cape Verdean Archipelago

„Falho de condições próprias que poderiam tornar rentável a exploração de um território geograficamente limitado e pequeno, o archipelago, se por um lado ganhou o justo epíteto de terra da fome, por outro, pela ausência dessas mesmas condições favoráveis, tornou-se o cadinho de uma rica experiência social (...) (França 1962: 7)."

---

forces, I argue, gave the Cape Verde archipelago an outsized role in Atlantic slavery's uneven decline and destruction. Some of these forces – the enforcement of anti-trafficking conventions, British abolitionist activity, the eclipsing of enslaved by free-labour in transatlantic labour flows – should be categorised as local echoes of a larger Atlantic narrative (Williams, D. 2015: 160)."

The objective of this article is to portray Cape Verdean society (being a very young culture that came into existence only in the 1460s) by means of its modern oral narrative manifested in form of myths/estórias. Although apparently in today's society a harmonic form of ethnic living-together seems to be installed in Cape Verdean everyday life, ambivalence with regards to perceiving and acknowledging African and European roots and influences still prevails in many aspects of individual and social existence.

The Cape Verdean Islands (la "Republica de Cabo Verde") is a nation on a volcanic archipelago off the northwest coast of Africa, 700 miles west of Dakar/Senegal. It's known for its Creole-Portuguese-African culture, traditional moma music that combines Blues with Latin American rhythms and melancholic Portuguese Fado and also for it's semi-arid climate.

The nine islands are spatially divided into two groups:
- The Barlavento Islands (windward islands, above the winds): Santo Antao, Sao Vicente, Santa Luzia, Sao Nicolau, Sal and Boa Vista and
- The Sotavento Islands (leeward, below the winds): Maio, Fogo (the active volcano, last eruption 2015), Brava and Santiago, home of the current capital Praia and of the old capital Ribera Grande).

Cape Verde is a land with very limited agrarian resources, permanent aridity (on most of the islands), a constant situation of water scarcity[2], and periods of depopulation

---

2   Nowadays the majority of goods has to be imported and there are only few desalination plants belonging to the bigger hotels.

by disease, starvation, and malnutrition. Some of the islands are completely deso-
lated and the 500.000 inhabitants have seen many periods of severe drought in the
past. In his story "Landflucht (rural depopulation)", Pedro Duarte describes scenes
of everyday life of the people in the old capital Ribera Grande during one of this
periods of dramatic aridity (cf. Duarte in Stauffer 2016: 11-21).

"The islands' broken topography and erratic rainfall were significant constraints
upon the emergence of an Atlantic plantation society. The flight of landed Africans
into the interior and the predations of pirates and disease placed additional limits on
the consolidation of a plantation society. Nevertheless, land use and the socio-eco-
nomic relationships among the titleholders of entailed estates (*morgados*), merchants,
rendeiros, mariners, *degregados*, *forros*, slaves, *lancados*, and maroons generated a
dynamic of hybriditiy, ladinization, and creolization that would make the archipelago, especially Santiago, an exemplary case study of Atlantic creole societies that
launched the Atlantic revolutions of sugar, tobacco, and rice (Williams 2015: 161)."
The historic centre of Ribera Grande was the first European colonial settlement
in the tropics. After the island was discovered by either Antonio da Noli or Diogo
Gomes (both are attributed with the discovery) in the 1460s, the settlement was
built in a valley inside a large stream named Ribera Grande and became an important port for trading slaves from Guinea Bissau and Sierra Leone to Brazil and the
Caribbean. Transcontinental slavery made the old capital that today is called Ribeira
Grande de Santiago[3] the second richest city in the Portuguese realm. It is home to
the eldest colonial church in the world – Nossa Senhora do Rosario – constructed

---

3   The name Cidade Velha was the city's name for many years, but since the name was considered
     discriminating it was substituted again by the old name Ribera Grande de Santiago in 2005.

in 1493-1495. In the historical course of the emerging Atlantic slave system however, the importance of Santiago and the other islands of Cabo Verde was apparently ephemeral in the larger arc of the Atlantic past (cf. Williams 2015: 161).

Due to its location on the maritime routes with the Americas and the South of Africa, the Cape Verdean archipelago had nevertheless great strategic importance and played a vital role in the rise of the Atlantic world. More than three centuries the islands were the pivot point of the trans-Atlantic slave trade (that had its roots in the older African slave trade), exile for political prisoners of Portugal[4], and place of refuge for the religiously persecuted during the Spanish-Portuguese inquisition. Further more it "remained a vital node for a multinational and multilingual assortment of people, information, and goods in north – south and east – west maritime transit (Williams 2015: 161)." The expansion of the Portugal global empire that (due to its inventions in ship-building) lasted around five centuries, began in the 14th century with the discovery of the Atlantic islands of Madeira and the Azores and with the establishment of trade posts and settlements along the African West coast. Some of them were fortified and far from local populations. In the middle of the fifteenth century, the Sotavento islands (Santiago and Fogo) served as testing grounds for early modern European maritime expansion in the Atlantic (cf. Williams 2015: 160). "The archipelago was drawn into a far-flung network of commerce, capital, labour, and ideology that connected to other Atlantic islands, Europe, and the Americas (Williams 2015: 161)."

The interpenetration of the two major cultural groups that formed the basic societal structures of the Cape Verdean islands, the "Europeans (above all the Portuguese)"

---

4   Political prisoners were also called "degradados"; often people did not want to emigrate to Africa.

and the "West-Africans" in their roles as colonizers and colonized, disembogued into the development of a Cape Verdean culture (o caboverdiano) and into a process of creolization (crioulização). Pidginization and creolization between the Portuguese and the Africans was allowed; ethnical mixture primarily occurred on the Atlantic islands of Cape Verde and Sao Tome that were colonized by a minority of Portuguese settlers and African slaves. The "Atlantic Creoles" as the historian Ira Berlin (1941) called West Africans who (from the 15th century onwards) also travelled as interpreters, negotiators and merchants on European merchant-ships and worked at the different trade posts and settlements. On the Cape Verdean islands families consisting of free men and women and slaves originated and a new Creole culture developed. Often European fathers didn't have a free wife and children, a situation that is said to have caused discomfort to many over the years. They all played a major role in the development of Pidgin and Creole languages allowing them to communicate with a big number of people from diverse mother languages. Of course people of different origin had to find own ways to communicate.

With the increase of collaboration between the Portuguese government and the British East India Company in 1838, the Cape Verdean islands experienced their second time of commercial florescence. With the construction of a floating coaling station at Porto Grande on São Vicente the archipelago became an important centre of coal storage, Mindelo[5] becoming the most relevant harbour. Permanent coaling facilities

---

5   "As the volume of the Atlantic economy grew, Mindelo grew as well, as the population rose from a
     mere handful in 1838 to more than 1400 by the 1860s. The inauguration of regular steamship service
     between Southampton and Rio, chartered to Royal Mail in 1851, and between Lisbon and Luanda,
     opened by the Empresa Lusitana that same year, renewed Cape Verde's status as a privileged enclave of
     passage and resupply within the modern Atlantic economy. Additional lines would be opened to British,
     French, German, and Italian enterprises by the 1870s, linking Cape Verde to major European, South

were built by British firms in 1850 and so the British crown began to exploit a steam route to the South Atlantic (cf. Williams 2015: 169). Mid of the nineteenth century "Cape Verde was a poor island colony that suffered from isolation, inadequate natural resources, harsh weather cycles, and an insecure labour force (Williams 2015: 163)." Many reports of those years refer to slave flight, especially in times of famine and disease, although the 1857 census gives notice of local slaveholders still managing to find the necessary means to maintain a creole's labour force (cf. Williams 2015: 163). Many Cape Verdeans started to emigrate to New England and found work in the whaling sector. Atlantic slavery was then selectively abolished in 1857 and in totality in 1878. Until the II World War the coal industry provided plenty of work for local labourers, but with the collapse of the economy this income source got reduced more and more and completely ended when the British coal industry went into decline in the 1980s.

After many years of struggle Cape Verde gained independence from Portugal on July 5, 1975. Parallely to an overall democratisation process in Sub-Saharan Africa, there was a strong demand for institutional changes in the 1980s, which eventually led to the installation of democracy in Cape Verde in the early 1990s. From the 1990s onwards then, Cape Verde embarked on a process of market-oriented economic reforms that already started at the end of the 1980s under the monopoly rule of the PAICV (Partido Africano da Independencia de Cabo Verde). With the victory of

---

American, and southern African ports. Mindelo served as a strategic fuelling station for punitive naval expeditions to the Cape Coast and the Indian Ocean. By the late 1800s, Mindelo was a bustling, sooty sin city inhabited by wage and contract labourers recruited from other islands (especially hardscrabble Santo Antão) and West Africa, Europeans in the employ of the coaling and steam packets companies, and itinerant crew and passengers (Williams 2015: 170)."

the MpD (Movimento para Democracia) in 1991, these reforms were widened and (cf. Bourdet 2000: 121).

"The economic reforms introduced in the early 1990s can be grouped under three main headings:

1) microeconomic measures whose aim is to improve the allocation of production resources and to spur economic growth. These first kinds of measures include the removal of price controls, the privatisation (or, if not viable, the liquidation) of a large number of state-owned enterprises (32 enterprises between 1994 and 1997), the strengthening of property rights in agriculture, the promotion of foreign direct investments, the revision of the Labour Code to increase labour market flexibility, and the modernisation of business legislation.

2) a market-oriented macroeconomic stance with the separation of fiscal and monetary policies (through the creation of a two-tier banking system) so as to give public policy the tools necessary for the conduct of stabilisation policy.

3) integration of the Cape Verdean economy into the world economy through the removal of quantitative restrictions on imports, the simplification and lowering of import tariffs, and the introduction of various export promotion measures, like the setting up of export-processing zones in Mindelho and Praia. These third kinds of measures also include a comprehensive tax reform whose aim is to broaden the tax base, improve the efficiency of the tax system and secure a level of tax revenue compatible with the development objectives of the government, as well as a nominal exchange rate peg (first to a currency and after July 1998 to the Portuguese escudo and indirectly to the euro), in order to build up antiinflationary credibility (Bourdet 2000: 122 f.)."

2. Language Usage on Cape Verde

Cape Verdean Creole belonged to the African subgroup that included besides the "Portugese criollos" of Cape Verde, those of Senegambia, Guines Portuguesa, São Tomé, Príncipe, Annobom and the "English criollos" of Sierra Leona (Krio) and Camerùn (cf. Granda 1974: 176). Cape Verdean Creole is known as the oldest African-European Creole language. It consists of approximately 90% of ancient Portuguese, the rest primarily of African (West African) languages, but also of aspects of French, English and other European languages. Mainly rhythm and graphic quality of Creole forms of expression stem from African languages. Cape Verdean Creole has no cases and no tenses; tenses are formed through attachments: I am=Nsta, I was=Nstaba.

Regarding the language use on the islands today, Portuguese is the official and the literary language, Creole is the national language, the "mother tongue" and the language of oral communication. "Sendo Cabo Verde um país monolingue, com urna lingua-máe crioula, (...)", writes Alberto Carvalho in his article *Narrativa cabo-verdiana, nacionalidade e nacionalismo* (cf. Carvalho 2001: 85).

While Portuguese is e.g. used in the media, in schools and in church, Creole is the colloquial language and is spoken in family circles, among friends and acquaintances. Further more it is the language of the arts and therefore also of the oral narrative of the archipelago. It is considered first language, so children usually arrive at their first day of school with only knowledge of Creole language. The transition to the school language Portuguese causes a lot of trouble. Since Creole was prohibited on the school grounds until Independence (5th July 1975), teachers may make use of Creole today in its support functions.

Two variants of Creole are being spoken:

1. the Crioulo de Sotavento (on the islands below the winds) and
2. the Crioulo de Barlavento (on the islands above the winds).

Myths/estórias are told orally in Creole languages and one of the central motifs is freedom which of course is related to the history of many centuries of slavery.

3.   Popular Cape Verdean Myths/Estórias

3.1   The Myth/Estória of the Ox Blimundo

(Source: cf. Pereira 2009: 10)

There are many myths/estórias on the islands, but there is one that is commonly known as the most popular of Cape Verdean historiography: The Estória of the OX BLIMUNDO. The estória of Blimundo has its origin in Santo Antao, in one the Islands above the winds (Barlavento) and is therefore transmitted mainly in Crioulo de Barlavento. Everyone on the Cape Verdean islands knows the story of Blimundo as we can read in the introduction of the famous Cape Verde artist Celina Pereira: "How good it feels to let us go by the sound of the wind of the leaves, by the fresh air inspiring our thoughts to run with no limit by our imagination. These are delicious and tasteful moments. How good it was to live again the beauty of 'Blimundo' so full of several symbolisms ending in an equal society utopia in the good sense of the word. This is the story of 'Blimundo' the true established myth of Cabo Verde historiography. And it carries with it the symbology of the social ascending of black people through love and music. And fresh images come to my memory of a beautiful childhood time while I listen to the sweet voices of the children singing the songs waving our dreams (cf. Vera Duarte, Education Minister Republic of Cabo Verde, in Pereira 2009: 1)."

Celina Pereira remembers the story the following way:
"Once upon a time there was an ox called Blimundo. Huge, beautiful, strong and so strong that every time he moo, the whole world trembled. He worked for a King at a sugar mill, which everyday around and around, made him feel more and more tired. He couldn't help thinking how to leave that 'slave job' which increased the richness of the king and the palace. The Queen and the Princesses had more and more beautiful clothes and the soldiers more shining uniforms. Blimundo says: 'I work harder everyday. My friends and I support this luxury... What can I do?'

One day, he escaped. He ran away from the palace far, far away... and the King was furious and decided that Blimundo should be caught. He mobilized all the soldiers saying that he wanted the ox back, dead or alive (better alive). And the first battalion left. The soldiers, very scared, descended and climbed rocks, trembling with Blimundo's moos... and did not resist his first kicks... One soldier was spared and returned to the palace to tell the King what had happened. Very angry with the lack of courage of his men, he ordered the departure of a second battalion, but they had the same destiny.

One day the Queen discovered 'the key' of the secret to make Blimundo return. 'He loves music...' – 'What?' – 'Music..., I am sure, and I know well the boy who used to play his ukulele... so let's send the boy to the fields...' And then the music boy knew another secret... namely that Blimundo was in love with 'codezinha' who was the most beautiful woman in the area... So the boy left, his ukulele in one hand, and in the other the meal the ox liked the most (popcorn) and a gourd filled with water. And he walked, descended, climbed... playing and singing... And he started to hear the moos, at first very far away, then coming closer...

Approaching more and more, he arrived next to Blimundo who was enchanted by the music. He said: 'Play more, closer to my ear! ...don't get to tired, climb on my neck!' From the top of Blimundo's body the song sounded better and better.

And they went on walking, walking, descending and climbing.. and descending... Nobody believed what they were seeing. Such a little boy with such a little instrument... everybody was astonished... it only could be a miracle! The King made Blimundo come in saying that the barber would prepare him for the wedding with his 'codezinha'. 'At least you get shaved'... but the barber was playing a game. Blimundo sat down, the towel around his neck, he was soaped and… then a cut of razor in the neck of Blimundo! But what happened? By the strength of Blimundo's kicks, the King flew away and disappeared forever… and our Blimundo went to live his freedom and the remembrance of his love in another land. And… amongst the rocks and valleys of the islands, the echoes still recall those sounds full of magic (Pereira 2009: 50-93)."[6]

(Source: cf. Pereira 2009: 76)

---

6   For the complete myth/estória of Blimundo cf. Pereira 2009: 50-93.

The myth/estória of Blimundo reflects on of the most central themes of Cape Verdean society, namely the vision of a just and equal society as well as the wish and longing for freedom, liberty and individual and collective independence. Since Cape Verde is a very young culture, the transmitted myths/estórias portray relevant values and societal needs.

3.2   The Myth/Estória of Ti Lobo y Chibinho and its Binomial Structures

The second most well known and popular myth/estória "Ti Lobo y Chibinho" has its origin on the islands "below the winds" (Islas de Sotavento) and many of them come from the island of Fogo, the last with a still active volcano.

Ti lobo, the ill-starred wolf from Cape Verde, has its counterpart in West Africa, but also in Europe. The animal wolf was never part of the Cape Verde fauna, but the goat-chibinho (also tobinho, sobrinho) in contrast is one of the most present existing animals. The wolf in many of the European stories is called "compadre/Gevatter/godfather" and he is usually accompanied by the fox. In Cape Verde the fox disappears and is replaced by the goat, sobrinho – chibinho (nephew). The motif of cousinship (compadrinho/Vetternschaft) is very popular in traditional Portuguese myths/estórias, but also in African narrative traditions from the Bantu and the Sudanese it can be found. By emphasizing this motif the memories of the African (sobrinho) and the European (compadre) matrices were integrated. "Ti lobo y chibinho (the wolf and the goat)" is one example of the myths/estorias transmitted

Folk-Lore from the Cape Verde Islands.

PART 1.

BY
ELSIE CLEWS PARSONS.

PUBLISHED IN CO-OPERATION WITH THE HISPANIC SOCIETY OF AMERICA.

CAMBRIDGE, MASS., AND NEW YORK:
PUBLISHED BY THE AMERICAN FOLK-LORE SOCIETY.
G. E. Stechert & Co., New York, Agents.
1923.

The American sociologist and anthropologist Elsie Clews Parsons (1875-1941) published a comprehensive work on the oral narrative of the Cape Verdean archipelago; her most famous book "Folk-Lore from the Cape Verde Islands" in which she collected stories from Cape Verdean immigrants scattered through eastern Massachusetts, Rhode Island and the seaports of Connecticut, was published in 1923 and is still considered one of the central books on the subject (cf. Parsons 1923). (Source: cf. https://en.wikipedia.org/wiki/Elsie_Clews_Parsons)

across generations in popular crioulo. There are many different combinations of animals such as "the rabbit and the hyena (from the Sudanese-Guinese tradition)", "The wolf (lobo) and the lamb (from the European tradition)", "the wolf and the goat (chibinho) (from the Cape Verdean tradition)", etc. Many European storytellers portrayed the wolf as a sort of super-beast that intimidated others. The mean wolf of the children's' fables often was represented as a wild animal and accused of being violent, sadist and cruel. Some interpretations considered the wolf the product of an archaic rite of initiation, transmitted through the oral tradition, including acts of provocation, keeping components of fear, darkness and hunger. Since the wolf was totally unknown on the archipelago, these characteristics became part of the Cape Verdean imagination. The concept got accentuated in the time of the slave trade when slave traders tried to profit from the superstition and supernatural belief many Africans had; so the traders introduced diverse "fears", also to hinder them from escaping at night. Often, from African stories' point of view, those who are naive and weak and in need to be protected, should not be victimized. Powerful animals though (like the European wolf or the African lion) can function as "monarchs", bringing justice to everyone. In many of the European stories in contrast, the stronger animals are often portrayed as mean, arrogant and oppressive, fighting against the weaker and helpless (cf. Carvalho (1986/?): 9 ff.).

In the myths/estórias of Ti Lobo y Chibinho we can observe a binomial structure that focuses on one-sided ascriptions of characteristics: one negative connotations, the other positive ones (cf. Filho 2002)[7].

---

7   In his article "As Estorias na Cultura Cabo-Verdiana (2002)" João Lopes Filho discusses the construction of the Cape Verdean society that he considers to be based upon a system of inequality. He describes the development of the oral tradition and the role of myths/estórias in the formation of Cape Verdean society and culture with special focus on the inherent binomial structures good-bad, order-disorder, above-below and hero-antihero.

Binomial Good/Bad

Binomial good/bad	Lobo	Chibinho
Social	• not existing in the archipelago • unknown, imagined • wild, raw force • destroys herds, other animals • lazy • transgressional behaviour	• exists in large numbers on the islands, known, real, domestic • clever and wise • hard working • respects the norms • integrates herds
Physical	• big • meager, hungry, insatiable, foodie • problems in articulating him-/itself	• small, moderate • well-fed, plump, saturated • articulates itself correctly
Psychological	• stupid, clumsy • imprudent, mean, impatient • ungrateful, egoist • cheats on the chibinho	• expert, knowledgeable • capable, canny, thoughtful • collaborative behaviour, dedicated • good, honest, unpretentious, wants to help the lobo

(Source: cf. Filho 2002: 59 f., translated by the author)

The animal with positive characteristics, representing the popular opinion, is the chibinho, who is also called sobrinho (nephew). On the one hand the stories refer to aggressive characters such as the wolf (lobo) or the hyena (hiena), on the other hand they give space for intimacy and relationship among the opponents paternity/ nephew, brotherhood/godfather. It seems like a description of balanced forces, a battle between good and bad. The disappearing aspects of aggression expresses a decrease of violence among the opponents and at the same time the appearance of intimacy and familiarity that creates a counterpoint to the idea of violence by bringing in the idea of non-violence. They are opposed to emphasize good social behaviour. The binomial order-disorder underlines a world-view of opposing forces circulating around human existential hardships (cf. Filho 2002: 59).

Binomial Order/Disorder

Disorder	Order
Situation of aridity and drought (frequent on the archipelago)	Water (wells, fountains)
↓	↓
Poverty, penury of food	Abundance of food (cane sugar, manioc)
↓	↓
Death (interrupts progress / erasure of populations)	Life (normal evolution)

(Source: cf. Filho 2002: 60, translated by the author)

Cape Verdeans belief that heaven is above at the firmament and that hell is in the inner of the earth; this world-view allows a construction of a system of opposites that are related (on CV funeral rites see also Saraiva 1998). A strong Christian influence can be found here. On the Cape Verde islands people try to find the divine in the protection against the spectrum of negative influences that has been persecuting them forever in form of stepmother Nature (natureza madastra) (cf. Filho 2002: 60).

Binomial Above/Below

Above	Below
Heaven	Earth
↓	↓
The divine world	The natural world
↓	↓
„nosso senhor", God (intermediary in the relatedness/connectivity of the two worlds)	„homem", human(s) (symbolically represented by the wolf (ti lobo))
↓	↓
The perfect (without fault, without criticism)	The imperfect (sinner, continuous violations of something, transgressions)

(Source: cf. Filho 2002: 61, translated by the author)

Also the presence of acoustic codes is significant, e.g. playing "lundu" or the "tambor" (symbol for the descent from heaven to earth), loin ribs that look like violin strings (symbol for hunger), bells celebrating marriage and showing abundant food. Every structure implies an anti-structure and allows a symbolic inversion. Strongly related to the traditional imagination, the transmutation of the subject in the myth-ological stories is not the result of superhuman intervention, but fruit of one's own cleverness and acumen to achieve certain objectives, to create points of convergence and "inversion", continuity and rupture, a similarity with the cosmos. Benevolence reminds of a gentleness which the lamb (cordeiro) is the symbol for, but also in its cleverness it approaches the smartness of the fox (raposa).

For the good behaviour the anthropomorphized "animal" assumes the role of the hero. The behavioural styles and the related virtues demonstrated in the stories can be differentiated into the models hero-antihero. The stories try to transmit virtues and values beneficial to the community; they show a cultural imprint of their contexts (cf. Filho 2002, whole article).

Binomial Hero/Anti-Hero

Hero	Anti-hero
• Chibinho (often a goat)	• Ti Lobo (wolf)
• Represents the „good" (bem)	• Represents the „bad" (mal)
• Defends moral values	• Practices immoral values
• Tries to realize sth.	• Tries to enrich oneself
• Follows principles	• Is disingenious

(Source: cf. Filho 2002: 62, translated by the author)

4.   Conclusion

By sharing the two myths/estórias of Blimundo and Ti Lobo & Chibinho I'd like to represent the young Cape Verdean culture and society with some of its main break lines and conflicts as well as its values, mores and identity-generating moment. Therefore myths/estórias of the archipelago cover the following aspects:

1. Relations between economic structures, social budgets and climatic conditions (drought, water scarcity)

2. Symbolic representations of the above describing primarily collective perceptions and imaginations

3. Myths/estórias can also show an internal conflict protecting the good vs. condemning the bad

4. Purpose of educating the younger generations:

    •   Mindful and moderate handling of resources

    •   Appropriate social behaviour

5. Therapeutic function and healing through a process of humanization and psychological integration (individuation[8])

As important oral cultural practice, the narration of myths/estórias – mostly in Cape Verdean Creole (crioulo) -, can be seen as a way to accompany processes of individuation and identification as well as a means to support identity-creation and -stabilization. Family and collective affiliation counterpoints the idea of violence

---

8   According to Jungian psychology, individuation is a process of psychological integration. Individuation is a process of transformation whereby the personal and the collective unconscious are brought into consciousness (by means of dreams, active imagination, free association) to be assimilated into the whole personality.

with the idea of non-violence. In the myths/estórias the disappearance of aggression is accompanied by the appearance of intimacy and familiarity. They play a role in the individuation process of individuals and communities. Further more as a pedagogical system the myths/estórias – such as "Ti Lobo" and "Blimundo" – can help Cape Verdeans to better understand the opposing sides and contrasts of social and personal life, to integrate their European and African past and to cope with everyday situations and big problems the archipelago was facing in the past and is still facing today.

References

Bourdet, Y. (2000): "Reforming the Cape Verdean Economy. The Economics of Mudança", in: *Africa Spectrum*, Vol. 35, No. 2, 121-163, Hamburg: Institute of African Affairs at GIGA.

Campbell-Badger, L. (2009): "A Selective and Annotated Bibliography of English and French Language Sources on Cape Verdean Literature", in: *Electronic Journal of Africana Bibliography* vol. 12. Available at: http://ir.uiowa.edu/ejab/vol12/iss1/1 (A phantastic collection of sources on Cape Verdean Literature; Email of Lindsey Campbell-Badger: lincampb@umail.iu.edu)

Carvalho, A. (1986): "Emergência do discurso na agressividade da poesia caboverdiana", in: *África, Literatura. Arte. Cultura.*, 2ª série, nº 14, ano 9, Lisboa, Ago.-Set.

Carvalho, A. (?, most probably 1986): "Sobre Literatura Oral Cabo-Verdiana", in: *Ciclo Cabo-Verdiano O Lobo e o Chibinho – Literatura-no-sitio*, pdf-formate, (?, no page numbers).

Carvalho, A. (2001): "A narrativa cabo-verdiana, nacionalidade e nacionalismo", in: *Revista de Filología Roniónica*, Anejos, 85-114.

Duarte, P. (2016): „Landflucht", in : Stauffer, Hans-Ulrich (Ed.), *Kapverden fürs Handgepäck*, Zürich: Unionsverlag, 11-21. (The book contains a selection of beautiful stories describing situations of Cape Verdean life and historical events through the centuries)

Filho, J. L. (2002): "As Estorias na Cultura Cabo-Verdiana", in: *Africana* n.° 25, Porto: Universidade Portucalense.

Franca, A. (1962): *Notas Sobre Poesia e Ficção Cabo-Verdianas*, Praia: Centro de Informação e Turismo.

Granda, G. de (1974): "Un posible modelo para la descripción sociolingüística de las hablas 'criollas' atlánticas, con especial atención a las del área hispanoamericana", in: *Zeitschrift für romanische Philologie, Zeitschrift für romanische Philologie* – 90, Aufsätze 29 Page(s), 174 – 202.

Parsons, E. C. (1923): *Folk-Lore from the Cape Verde Islands,* Cambridge: American Folk-Lore Society.

Pereira, C. (2009): *Estória, Estória... Do Tambor a Blimundo* (Illustrations by Roberto Chichorro), Caparica: Publicar, LDA. (The audio-book by Celina Pereira contains some of the most popular myths/estórias of Cape Verde)

Saraiva, M. C. (1998): "Rituais Funerarios em Cabo Verde: permanência e inovação", in: *Revista da Faculdade de Ciências Sociais e Humanas,* n.º 12, Lisboa: Edições Colibri, 121-156.

Williams, D. (2015): "Cape Verde at the End of Atlantic Slavery", in: *Slavery & Abolition,* 36:1, 160-179.

II

PATAKÍ (PATAKINES) AND DIVINATION SYSTEMS IN CUBA AND THEIR FOUNDATION IN THE IFÁ ORACLE

Abstract

Cuban culture, its people and their customs and belief systems are based on European, African and indigenous American influences. Despite the fact that Cuba is primarily considered a Catholic country – around sixty percent of the population are followers of the Catholic Church -, it is still home to other large religions and/or mythologies that developed or continued to exist in different forms on the island. According to the two major Cuban ethnic groups, namely la lucumí (Western African origin) y la conga (Central African origin) – yoruba y bantu -, the following "religious" groups can be differentiated: Santería or Regla de Ochá, La Regla de Ifá or Lucumí (Yoruba) and Palo Monte or Las Reglas de Congo, La Regla de Mayombe, in short regla lucumí and regla conga (cf. Cabrera 1993: 70). The word regla can be translated with cult, religion or spiritual belief system; it refers to rites and religious and magical practices that during the colonial times were imported from African countries and over time have been altered or changed or became syncretized with Catholicism.

Due to Eurocentric tendencies during the colonial era as well as during the time of the early Republic, Afro-Cuban religions and mythologies were often negatively

associated with black magic and witchcraft. "West African-derived Santería is generally a highly regarded Cuban cultural treasure, whereas, Palo Monte is typically
regarded with suspicion. Although Santería shares the same persecutory history as all
African-identified subjects its contemporary representation is more favourable than
its Central African counterpart (Scott 1999: 13)." The major focus of this article is
put on the Yoruba culture and the Santería tradition.

The cults are based on traditional and largely secret, still orally transmitted myths.
Any attempt to canonize these cults in writing has – often – failed so far, because
there is no institution that decides on right or wrong practice of religion. Nowadays
all over Cuba specific cults are being practised. This is especially true for the Abakuá-society as well as for the Arará and Yorubá, whose mythic forms are popularly
known as Patakí or Patakines which are mythological stories, morals, legends, and
parables; oral and written narratives that have been inherited from the African ancestors. "They date back to ancient times like the world itself and have certain links
with all what exist – animals, plants, human beings and even the orishas themselves.
These stories are transmitted by Ifá priests, olúos, babalawos, obbás, oriatés, iyaloshas, and etc., by means of cowry shells, odduns or Ifá signs; actually, many of these
patakines are included in the popular speech and we take their wise advices. They
are the most important part of the consultations made by iyaloshas and babalawos
due to the fact that they are red and interpreted for both, from them emerge what
the saints and orishas want to tell us or show us and, although many of them are
alike, none have the same meaning. The main point is the interpretation we are
able to make and bring to our daily life (Gómes Nieves 2016: 5)." These mostly still
orally transmitted myths in form of simple stories could be spread across the island

and therefore come to vernacular esteem with also practical and secular use for daily life (cf. Barnet 2000: 9 f.).

Another herewith related prevalent mythological Cuban tradition are the divination systems used in Afro Cuban religious practices that are, as Barnet emphasizes, based upon a polymorphic mythological foundation. Every sign or formula belonging to one of the divination systems such as the system of throwing cocos (*tirada del coco*), throwing cowrie shells (*tirada de los caracoles, Diloggun*) or to the system of Ifá panels (*tablero de Ifá*) presumes one or more stories or patakí/patakines offering advice to those seeking advice. In most cases the protagonists are the gods themselves giving advice or providing help, but also natural forces and animals can play an important role. So many patakí/patakines organize human interaction and living together (cf. Barnet 2000: 11 ff.). Both, Patakí/patakines and divination systems are based upon a mythological foundation.

The basic idea of the article is to illustrate how the present major Cuban divination system had originated and how it is being practiced today. Above all it shall be shown how the Cuban system emerged from the larger African system.

1.   Facts and Thoughts related to the History of Cuba, the Period of Atlantic Slavery and the Reality of the African Diaspora

So representing the reality of Cuba as a closely knit network of diverse roots of its inhabitants became a common trait of Cuban society. Gastón Baquero writes: "In the New World, from the sixteenth century to today and forever, three basic human groups lived together (in Cuba): the group of those who were there, those who came to settle down and those who have come by force. Indians, Europeans and Africans who were forced to live together ... If their blood was mixed or not, their souls, their words, their beliefs and their superstitions, their customs and their feelings mingled". The name Cuba in Taino language means large land, well sown, and the first socio-cultural Cuban model was the aboriginal, namely the Arawak people of the Tainos and Subtainos as well as the Ciboneyes. The second socio-cultural Cuban model was formed by the Spanish and the African cultures.

For a period of two hundred years the "Black Caribbean"[9] – as Alexander von Humboldt had named the Caribbean Sea and the Gulf of Mexico – was a focal point of slavery; on the neighboring islands Jamaika, Saint-Domingue/Haiti and Cuba sugar production with mass slavery flourished from 1680 to 1880. With the massive slave trade many people from the African continent arrived to the Caribbean. The centers of the slave trade shifted to the west and north at the end of the 18th century and

---

9   In one of his major works, the essay on the island of Cuba (1826), Alexander von Humboldt described a "black Caribbean" with about 80 percent descendants of Africans. Albert Wirz (1984) wrote that until the 19th century America was an extension of Africa, as the number of Africans living there exceeded that of white by several times (cf. Zeuske 2003: 25).

so Cuba became the most efficient and compact slavery in the Western world since the early 19th century. Slavery of the "Big Cuba (Cuba Grande)" which was the centre of this Caribbean had its roots in the Indian history of the Caribbean, in the Spanish Conquista and in the history of Havana as an Atlantic World Harbor and slave trading center. The Antilles metropolis Havana was considered the undisputed queen of the Black Caribbean in the 19th century, her glory, wealth and shine being based on slave smuggling, slavery and trade (cf. Zeuske 2003: 23).

Many of the ancestors of today's islanders came from the Iberian Peninsula (14th -18th centuries), in the first half of the 18th century from the African countries, especially from the areas south of the Sahara (from the Niger Basin, Ivory Coast, Congo and Angola, Dahomey (today Benin), Nigeria and the region that extends from today's Senegal to Liberia). The African groups mostly came from the ethnic groups of the Bantú and the Yorubá, but also from other ethnic communities such as the Achantil, the Bambará, the Congo, the Fulbé, the Ibibió and the Malinqué. During the 16th and 17th centuries – until slavery got abolished on October 7 in 1886 – about approximately one Million African slaves were brought to Cuba as part of the Atlantic slave trade. By 1789, the year in which slave trade was released by the Spanish Crown, already approximately 50.000-60.000 African slaves had reached Cuba. Around 8,7 % of the displaced people from Africa were brought to Cuba (between 1821 and 1860 appr. 350.000 people). From 1860 until 1880 Cuba had the whole Atlantic-Slave Trade for itself (cf. Zeuske 2018: 201).

With the beginning of the Atlantic slave trade[10] – a "forced globalization (Zeuske

---

10   The Atlantic slave trade is being distinguished from other contemporary trade forms such as the East-African slave trade, the Mediterranean slave trade and the inner-African slave trade.

2003: 24)" so to say was initiated -, high numbers of people were robbed, enslaved and deported from their home countries in West, Central and South Africa. Estimations go up to 12 million people who in the course of time became victims of the Atlantic slave trade (cf. Segal 1995: 4). With the expansion, European agents and haulers have swung up themselves to masters of the sea and therewith during the modern era established the Atlantic slavery. In the beginning of the Atlantic phase between 1450 and 1521 approximately 156.000 people were displaced by the Portuguese, mostly in inner-African economic cycles. After 1526 the slave shipments reached Cuba directly from Africa. Only a smaller number reached Europe or the early America, most were brought to the West-African islands controlled by the Iberians. For example in 1552 around 3.000 Cativos were sent to Madeira and at that time represented 15% of the population, whereas mid of the 16th century approximately 11.400 came as slaves to the Cape Verdean islands where they made 90% of the population (cf. Zeuske 2018: 190 ff.). During the 16th and 17th centuries – as already mentioned – about approximately one Million African slaves were brought to Cuba as part of the Atlantic slave trade.[11] Between 1650 and 1750 – as proven by statistic documentation[12] – in the number of African slaves outside of Africa became the dominant fraction of the global slave population. Zeuske calls the Portuguese and the mostly in Africa living Atlantic Creoles the "masters of all

---

11   Cf. https://en.wikipedia.org/wiki/Slavery_in_Cuba
12   „Schon ältere Statistiken weisen aus, dass britische Kapitäne, Kaufleute, Schiffsausrüster und Investoren sowie Kapitalanleger in der Neuzeit, besonders von 1650 bis 1807, Menschen meist in Afrika gekauft oder eingetauscht haben, um sie über den Atlantik in die relativ kleinen englischen Kolonialterritorien der Amerikas zu bringen, mit einem absoluten Höhepunkt in den Jahren 1781 bis 1800. In dieser Zeit nahem das britische Parlament, das heute vorwiegend für den *Slave Trade Act* (Verbote des Sklavenhandels auf britischen Schiffen) von 1807 erinnert wird, noch Pro-Sklaverei- und Pro-Sklavenhandels-Gesetze an (Zeuske 2018: 193)."

European-Atlantic slave traders"; Portugal respectively Brazil had displaced around 5,8 million people to the Americas, still less than the British who had displaced around 3,2 million people from Africa (cf. Zeuske 2018: 194 f.).

The "corporeal capitalism (Kapitalismus menschlicher Körper)" of the Trans-Atlantic-Slave Trade[13] was a successful and flourishing business, counting – according to the enclosed database from 2011 – approximately 12.521.336 million enslaved people by European states. In 1969 Philipp Curtin already found out that 11 to 12 million Africans, mostly men and boys, had been displaced to the Americas between 1501 and 1868 (cf. Zeuske 2018: 196).[14]

Focusing on the Trans-Atlantic-Slave Trade to Cuba and Brazil, it can be said that altogether around 8,7 % of the displaced people from Africa were brought to Cuba. About 1810 the ports of Rio, other Brazilian cities, La Habana and other Cuban cities, received ca. 58 % of the Atlantic Slave-Trade (Cuba 19 %, Brazil 39 %). In 1830 43 % reached Cuba and 44 % Brazil, whereas in 1850 already 92 % of the trade focused on Cuba and only 4 % on Brazil. As said from 1860 until 1880 Cuba was the central location of the Atlantic-Slave Trade (cf. Zeuske 2018: 201).

---

13   One important alternative historical perspective came into the picture by Gilroy's book about a distinct black Atlantic culture that incorporated elements from African, American, British, and Caribbean cultures. The idea of the *Black Atlantic* was introduced by Paul Gilroy in 1993: "In The Black Atlantic, Gilroy puts forward the idea that 'cultural historians could take the Atlantic as one single, complex unit of analysis' and 'use it to produce an explicitly, transnational and intercultural perspective' (15) (Evans 2009: 255)." In his work *The Black Atlantic: Modernity and Double Consciousness* (1993) he introduces the idea of "double consciousness" as a means of negotiating being "both European and black" and hereby challenges existing ethnically absolutist discourses representing these identities as 'mutually exclusive' (cf. Evans 2009: 255). But of course "black modernity" is much broader than the traumatic history of slavery and has 'many inflections' resonating beyond the experiences of slaves and their descendants.

14   Zeuske believes that people smuggling continued until 1880 (cf. Zeuske 2018: 196).

Creolization became a positively connotated sociocultural model of living together within the context of the African Diaspora; Mintz and Price introduced the model of Creolization in the 1970ies (cf. Rauhut 2012: 45).[15] The Creolization model was criticized by Thornton (1992), Gilroy (1993) and Lovejoy (2000) who represented the so-called Atlantic Approach that comprehends the Atlantic world as analyser and puts the diverse historic and contemporary interactions between Africa, the Americas and Europe in the centre of focus (cf. Rauhut 2012: 45).[16] The central idea of the "African Diaspora Studies" after 1990 was the consideration of mutual developments on both sides of the Atlantic as well as to increase the visibility of a "Black History". Since the 1950ies the term African Diaspora is being used by black intellectuals in the USA. Following Gilroy's Atlantic Approach many authors pled for a stronger recognition of the until today existing effective dimensions of African history and presence beyond slavery and into the living environments of the Diaspora-societies (cf. Lovejoy 2000, Palmie 1995b) (cf. Rauhut 2012: 47). Gilroy's approach was also criticized for its one-sided orientation towards Anglophone Western societies (cf. Dorsch 2000: 168) and its over-emphasis of blackness and Africanness by ignoring multi-cultural realities of the respective societies at the same time (cf. Zeleza 2005: 7, 63) (cf. Rauhut 2012: 47).

Africa does not always represent the idealized and lost homeland to which many people would like to symbolically return to. In fact a strong identity positioning

---

15   „Stattdessen haben sich nämlich neue, afroamerikanische Kulturen herausgebildet (Mintz/Price 1976; Mintz/Price 1992) (Rauhut 2012: 45)."
16   See also Shepperson (1966, 1982), Harris (1982, 1996: 14) on "mobilized black diaspora", Clifford (1994, 1997) on "travelling cultures", Hall (1994: 26 ff.) on the "production and making of an imaginary African centre in Caribbean black diaspora" (cf. Rauhut 2012: 46).

occurs within the creolized, syncretized context of Caribbean and Latin-American societies. Over time many different cultural and religious influences reached the island and got syncretized, e.g. Spanish Catholicim, Haitian Vodoo[17], Judaism and Islam, North American Protestantism and Spiritualism and a conjunct ot African religions that will be focused upon in more detail later on. When the family bonds of the to Cuba displaced Africans broke and their system of relations completely dissolved, the cults had to reorganize themselves and adapt to the Cuban environment and society which led to a very specific process of transculturation related to the worship of specific gods and goddesses, forms and objects of cults and religious beliefs (cf. Barnet 2000: 8).

Cuban babalawos often consider Cuba the centre of an African religious authenticity, not necessarily Africa. This conceptual fuzziness is also valid for the Yoruba-Diaspora. The Yoruba themselves are the result of a ethno-historical construction through Christian mission and colonial rule (cf. Falola, Childs 2004: 4); the Yoruba-Diaspora is based on the following components: the experience of slavery, the return movement to West Africa since the 1850ies, the conscious attribution of the Yoruba-Diaspora via religion in diverse local and global references (cf. Falola, Childs 2004: 8,10) (cf. Rauhut 2012: 48 ff.). The Diaspora-consciousness through religion means that the Yoruba-Diaspora constitutes itself through the global devotees of religions such

---

17   Against the compulsory globalizations of the 18th and 19th centuries, the largest slave revolution in world history broke out on the French Caribbean colony of Saint-Domingue in 1791. Saint-Domingue disappeared from the map and Haiti appeared – from 1822 to 1843, Haiti encompassed the entire island of Santo Domingo (cf. Zeuske 2003: 24). In the wake of the revolutionary slave revolt in Haiti in 1791, many French landowners who had owned sugar and coffee plantations there fled to Cuba. Under their influence and with their technical knowledge, Cuba became for Spain what Haiti had previously been for France: the island of sugar and coffee. Economic upswing and the industrial use of slaves were the result (cf. https://de.wikipedia.org/wiki/Geschichte_Kubas).

as the Santería, Candomblé and Orisha-Voodoo. It is therefore questionable if the points of origin of these religions (Havanna, Bahia, New York, Miami, etc.) can still be called Diaspora, since they have generated original and independent religions and form points of intersections from where these religions through globalization and migration have spread all over the world in the last forty years (cf. Rauhut 2012: 52).

2.   Religion and Cuban Society

Cuba's religious and spiritual culture can be described as a Christian African Syncretism, the major religious traditions today being:

- La Regla de Ocha Ifá (Regla Lucumi) or Santería from the Yoruba speaking people (Lucumi is the liturgical language of the Santería): the most significant system in Cuba. Alliance with the Yoruba culture (Nigeria, Benin). The system is composed of the "Regla Ocha", the Orixá cult and the priesthood of Ifá. The "Regla Ocha" and Ifá include complex divination systems, ancestor veneration and different levels of initiation (e.g. el Benbe – fiesta de Santo).

- Palo Monte or Regla de Mayombe (Regla Conga) from the Bantu speaking people: has its origin in the Bantú Pueblos. Its belief system is based on ancestor veneration and on the power of the nkinsis (spirits, or an object that a spirit inhabits). Centre of the cult is around the nganga (a Kikongo language term for herbalist or spiritual healer – in Cuba, the term *nganga* refers to a certain creation made with an iron cauldron into which several items such as bones and sticks are placed. It also refers to the spirit of the dead that resides there. In Palo, it refers to an iron cauldron used to venerate the mpungo which can be used for magic and divination. There is a strong focus on medical knowledge as well as on healing with herbs and plants.

• La Regla de Arara fromt the Arara Dahomey, a less popular tradition, and Los Ñáñigos o Abakuá: ceremonies around the sacred "tambor Ekue" and the figure of the sacred "fish Tanze". Origins: region of Calabar (today Nigeria) (cf. Tamajo 2018).

Two African religions in Cuba were and are dominant: the Lucumí and the Congo religion (cf. Barnet 2000: 84). The Lucumí (la lucumí) are of Western African origin, the Congo (la conga) of Central African origin, yoruba being the language and culture of the Lucumí and bantu the one of the Congos. In consequence two cults or religious orientations manifested in Cuba: the Santería or Regla de Ochá, also called La Regla de Ifá or Lucumí (Yoruba) and Palo Monte or Las Reglas de Congo, also called La Regla de Mayombe – in short the two cults are named regla lucumí and regla conga (cf. Cabrera 1993: 70).

In Cuba, the Yorubá culture enjoys the strongest influence of all originally "immigrant" African cultures, not least because of the practice of their popular religion, called "Regla de Ocha" or "Santería". According to the theory of the Cuban school, la Santería is composed of two cults, the Regla de Ocha (cult of Ocha) and the Regla de Ifá (cult of Ifá). The first stands for the practice of santeros and santeras, the second for the practice of babalawos and santeros mayores. In the daily religious activities such as the methodology of divination, the realization of rituals and ceremonies, the worship of deities, the expression of language and cultural manifestations, both practices are very similar and their structures are closely intertwined (cf. Delgado Torres 2005: 21). As already mentioned, the article focuses on the Santería tradition.

3.   Cuban Santería
(Regla de Ochá, Regla de Ifá, Regla Lucumí)

La Santería is a conjunct of beliefs that is expressed in a cult for the 401 deities of their pantheon, adored by the yoruba population which consists of different groups of people such as the priests of Ifá, the Regla de Ocha and its priests as well as other religious followers, families, etc. The cult/religion is practised in many countries and cultures.[18] According to the theory of the Cuban school, la Santería is composed of two cults, the Regla de Ocha (cult of Ocha) and the Regla de Ifá (cult of Ifá). The first stands for the practice of santeros and santeras[19], the second for the practice of babalawos[20] and santeros mayores[21].In the daily religious activities such as the methodology of divination, the realization of rituals and ceremonies, the worship of deities, the expression of language and cultural manifestations, both practices are very similar and their structures are closely intertwined (cf. Delgado Torres 2005: 21).[22]

Major forms of expression used by the Santería practitioners are: lithology or the stones, hydrology or the waters, flora and fauna, liturgy, theological literature, parapsychology,

---

18   Variants of the cult/religion yoruba are for example: Candomblé, Ketu (Brazil), Oyotunji (United States), Kélé (Saint Lucia), Quimbanda (Brazil), Santería (Cuba), Trinidad Orisha (Trinidad), Umbanda (Brazil), Yoruba religion (Nigeria) (cf. https://en.wikipedia.org/wiki/Santer%C3%ADDa).

19   Santeros/santeras can be translated by those who are devoted to saints, also as priests of the santería as known in Cuba

20   Babalawo can be translated as father of the mysteries

21   Santeros mayores can be translated as senior priests

22   The development of the santería in Cuba was influenced and determined by two major generations evolving into the two contemporary streams of Regla de Ocha and Regla de Ifá: 1. the group of santeros including Atanda, Akunko, Fa Bi, Kainde, Ifá Omi, Olugere, Ade Lokun, Adechina; 2. the group of santeros including Miguel Febles, José Antonio Erice, Bonifacio Valdés, Juan Angulo, Valentín Cruz, Facundo Sevilla, Ramón Febles, Bernardo Roja, Quintín García, Juan Antonio Ariosa, Miguel Iznaga, Arturo Peña, Martín Cabrera, Arecelio Iglesias, etc. (cf. Delgado Torres 2015: 22 f.).

green and traditional medicine, dance and music as well as other art forms (cf. Delgado Torres 2015: 23). As Alexis Valdés emphasizes in his prologue to the work of Delgado Torres (2005), the term "Santería" has often been used in the past in an inadequate way and therefore it has happened that many times it has been misinterpreted as magic or witchcraft ("brujería") expressed with a negative connotation (cf. Torres 2005: 1f, cf. Efundé 1978: 7). Nevertheless the Cuban followers have continued using the term.

4.   The traditional Ifá Oracle and Divination System

4.1   The roots of the Cuban Ifá Oracle and divination system

The roots of the Cuban Ifá Oracle and divination system can be traced back to the ancient African "Ifá Oracle[23] or Divination System" that is still being practiced in Togo, Nigeria and Benin. It had originated in Yorubaland[24] (in Yoruba: Ile-Yoruba),

---

23   There are different techniques and philosophies for communicating with the spiritual world. On the one hand the inner path (meditation, contemplation), on the other hand the outer path via the spiritual interpretation of the external world (astrology, numerology, etc.) or via the direct communication with the spiritual world (divination techniques, oracles, channelings, etc.).The oracle's advantage lies in the ability to learn and pass on knowledge as well as in the differentiated derivation of knowledge and approaches. It is an instrument for analyzing a situation from a spiritual point of view as well as for deriving recommendations for action. Oracles provide information about the options for decision making, tips on qualities, and whether certain aspects are in balance, whether access to internal qualities is present or blocked. The oracle is closely interwoven with other mystical elements such as the magic, the dance, the cult of the forefathers and various forms of incorporation. indirect communication about the oracle or very direct communication with mental entities (cf. Plöger 2016: 29 ff.).

24   The Yorubaland (Yoruba: Ile-Yoruba), lies in the Southwestern part of Nigeria. Yoruba is the second largest language group in Africa, consisting of over 20 million people. The term „Yoruba", according to Frank A. Salamone (2010:319), „encompasses about twenty-five separate groups, each one culturally different from the other". The people trace their origin or descent to a great ancestor, Oduduwa, who came from Ile-Ife. The bulk of the people are today found in Ogun, Ondo, Oyo, Lagos, Ekiti and

formerly part of the Southwestern area of Nigeria, where Ifá is a major divinity that is closely identified with Yoruba history, mythology, religion and fold medicine. The word Ifá refers to the mystical figure Ifá or Orunmila, regarded by the Yoruba as the deity of wisdom and intellectual development. William Bascom emphasizes: „Ifá is the most respected, in many ways the most interesting, system of divination of five to ten million Yoruba in Nigeria (1969, ix) (214)." So Ifá is an important system of divination found in many cultures of West Africa. Nowadays it is practiced among Yoruba communities and by the African Diaspora in the Americas and the Caribbean. As well in the original as in the Cuban system "Ifá is a type of historical poetry – Ifá divination poetry is regarded as a record of the activites of the divinities and the ancestors on earth (Abimbola 1977: 21)." It is firstly an oracle, secondly a divination system and thirdly a corpus of philosophical and liturgical knowledge consisting of thousands of transmitted verses. The Oracle of Ifá is the core of the whole mythological system holding its world view.

Within the Santería ifism[25] (el ifismo) can be considered the superior theology; it

---

substantial parts of Kwara and Kogi state bound together by language, traditions and religious beliefs and practices. Islam, Christianity, and the „traditional" Yoruba pantheon, the Orisa, are all embraced in Yorubaland. The bond shared by all Yoruba people is the centrality of ritual to specific occasions, as well as to everyday life. The keynote of the life of the Yoruba is their religion. However, ample information on traditional Yoruba religions exists (Talbot, 1932; Bascom, 1941; Lucas, 1948; Evans-Pritchard, 1965; Idowu, 1962; Gleason, 1973; Mbiti, 1975; Abimbola, 1976). These religions are „primordial" among the various Yoruba communities because many of them are timeless for they are centuries old, while the beliefs and worships associated with them constitute traditional ideologies and tap roots of ethnic culture. According to Idowu (1962:5), religion forms the foundation and the all governing principle of life for them. The full responsibility of all the affairs of life belongs to the deity as far as they are concerned.

25   Ifism is a spiritual tradition that encompasses similarities of spiritual African Yoruba traditions that originated in the areas of today's Nigeria, Togo, Benin. The spiritual principles have not been written down, but were orally passed on in form of verses as part of the Oracle of Ifa. Ifism incorporates majorly the orally transmitted verses of the Oracle of Ifa. Later they were passed on as mythological stories in form of narrations. For the understanding and practice of all rituals they are from fundamental and crucial

is described as a conjunct of theological treatises containing the respective maxims corresponding to the theory and practice of the priests of Ifá or the *babalawos* (cf. Delgado Torres 2005: 22). Ifism is a monotheistic system that teaches a pantheon of spiritual entities possessing defined energetic qualities. These qualities and links are recited in form of Itans (mythological verses), often sung or narrated.[26]

In 2008 the Ifá Divination System was inscribed on the Representative List of the Intangible Cultural Heritage of Humanity (originally proclaimed in 2005):

"The Ifá divination system, which makes use of an extensive corpus of texts and mathematical formulas, is practiced among Yoruba communities and by the African diaspora in the Americas and the Caribbean. The word Ifá refers to the mystical figure Ifá or Orunmila, regarded by the Yoruba as the deity of wisdom and intellectual development. In contrast to other forms of divination in the region that employ spirit mediumship, Ifá divination does not rely on a person having oracular powers but rather on a system of signs that are interpreted by a diviner, the Ifá priest or babalawo, literally "the priest's father". The Ifá divination system is applied whenever an important individual or collective decision has to be made. The Ifá literary corpus, called odu, consists of 256 parts subdivided into verses called ese, whose exact number is unknown as they are constantly increasing (there are around 800 ese per odu). Each of the 256 odu has its specific divination signature, which is determined by the babalawo using sacred palm-nuts and a divination chain. The ese, considered the most important part of Ifá divination, are chanted by the priests in poetic language. The ese

---

importance – without them it is impossible. Ifism sees human beings involved in constant development processes from dark to light; objective is to become a good person, to come into the world to bless the earth.

26   Anselmo Suárez y Romero (1818-1878) published a work on the oral literature of the slaves in Cuba, the *Canciones de los negros* (1853).

reflect Yoruba history, language, beliefs, cosmovision and contemporary social issues. The knowledge of Ifá has been preserved within Yoruba communities and transmitted among Ifá priests. Under the influence of colonial rule and religious pressures, traditional beliefs and practices were discriminated against. The Ifá priests, most of whom are quite old, have only modest means to maintain the tradition, transmit their complex knowledge and train future practitioners. As a result, the youth and the Yoruba people are losing interest in practising and consulting Ifá divination, which goes hand-in-hand with growing intolerance towards traditional divination systems in general (cf. UNESCO intangible world heritage, https://ich.unesco.org/en/RL/ifa-divination-system-00146; Ifa Group of Oyo, text & films 2004/2008/2009)."

Therefore Ifá is seen as a "repositary of beliefs and moral values – it is regarded the voice of the divinities and wisdom of the ancestors (cf. Abimbola 1977: preface V)." The Ifá divination system and the extensive poetic chants associated with it are used by the Yoruba to validate important aspects of their culture. Ifá divination is performed by the Yoruba during all their important rites of passage such as naming and marriage ceremonies, funeral rites and installation of kings. Generally speaking the authority of Ifá permeated every aspect of life, because Ifá is regarded the voice of the divinities and wisdom of the ancestors (cf. Abimbola 1977: preface V). Ifá occupies a kingly position among the Yoruba divinities. Through the Ifá divination system human beings can communicate with the divinities and the ancestors. Ifá is more than a Yoruba system. Its traces can be found in several other West African cultures: Edo, Igbo, Ewe, Fon, Nupe, Borgu, etc.) (cf. Abimbola 1977: 15).[27]

---

27   The system follows the oral transmission: learning of poems and informal training. The trainee learns
      while sitting by his master watching how he manipulates the Ifa instruments and how he chants the

The mythology of Ifá has its base in the **Yoruba Pantheon** (inspired by/cf. Plöger 2016: 50 ff.):

Yoruba Pantheon

Olodumare (The Supreme God) – threefold: Olorun/Eledumare/Olofi
gave **emi** (breath of life) to humankind

↓

Orixa Oxala (masculine side/spiritual world)
& Orixa Odudua (feminine side/material world)
Orunmila (=Ifa – entity of spiritual communication, divination)

Orixás (positive entities) / Odús (structures)   - "karma-free level"
Obbatala, Chango, Oboluare, etc.

↓

Can manifest and – for a limited period of time - take control over
consciousness and movements of a dancer (Plöger 2016: 50/51)

Eggúngun/Eguns - Ancestors (ancestrial worship, ancestral shrine) -   **"karma**
                        Egbe (heavenly comrads)   **level"**
Material world/
Many life-forms (entities) – material/non-material

There is negativity and positivity in this universe – neg. and pos. are twins. The Orixá Esu can go to
the right and to the left (representation of the Universe).

Ifa poems to his clients. Also he learns the sacrifices which go with each poem. Also about medicine. Initiation forms the climax of many years of studies. The training of a Ifa priest starts at the age of ten or twelve. The student remains with their master for the next ten-fifteen years. In average it takes two to three years to learn the names of the 256 Odu and their signatures (cf. Abimbola 1977: 12). A Babalaô (Baba=father, Awo=mystery) is "the custodian of mystery", it is the name for a priest in the Santeria or the in Regla de Ocha-Ifa; in Regla de Mayombe or Palo Monte the priest's name is Padre Nganga or Taita Inkisi. The education of a true babalawo is a life-long process.

In the beginning was Olodumare (the Almighty, all-knowing and ever-existing God) who created heaven (orun) and earth (aye) and separated them. Olodumare gives tasks to his entities, the Odus and Orixas, keeps material and spiritual worlds together and delimits them from each other. Olodumare does not interfere in life, but structures the basic principles and implements through his entities. The world unfolds from unity, in the first phase as self-unfolding duality/polarity in form of a god-father and god-mother develops in Yoruba mythology: Oxala and Odudua (the first Orixas) – all spiritual principles are being passed on via sung prayers (orikis) and sacred verses (itans).[28] Itan are archetypical principles such as Yoruba religious beliefs, sacred verses and narrations revealing themselves in the Oracle (cf. Plöger 2015: 43). Oxala is the first entity of the Orixa-pantheon and stands for the masculine side, for the spiritual world. Orixas originate from and with Oxala. Odudua represents the feminine side of god, the material world (cf. Plöger 2016: 41).

Olodumare exists in three forms or manifestations (primordial trinity):

- Olorun: associated with the sun, is the ruler of (or in) the heavens, creator of ashe (life energy) and the Orixas;
- Eledumare: the creator god, creator of the Universe, the world and life;
- Olofi: is the ruler of the Earth, mediator between orun (heaven, the spiritual realm) and aye (earth, the material realm) (cf. Plöger 2016: 41).

Entities occupying the karma-free level of the spiritual world are the following:

- The Orixas (divinities/qualities) of the spiritual world and relations between these qualities, reflected and mirrored in the material world (plants, animals, objects, symbols, etc. – in healing, magic, dance, prayer relevant): created the earth and

---

28   The Yoruba differentiate two classes of tales, 1.) folktales (alo) and 2.) myths and legends (itan).

life on earth. Olodumare gives live-breath to human beings, the Orixas shape communication between human beings and the spiritual world.

- Odus define the paths and energy structures of the Universe on which human beings wander. These qualities and links are recited in form of itans (mythological verses), often sung or narrated. The Yoruba believe that the Odu are divinities in their own right who had descended from orun into the city of Ife and that they were sent by Oludumare to replace Orunmila on earth after the return of the latter to orun (cf. Plöger 2016: 42 ff.).

4.2   The Archetypes of Ifá

In the Ifá -tradition it is believed that human beings are essentially led by three entities:

- Everything comes out of a single god Olodumaré (monotheistic worldview)
- Orixás are spiritual entities that determine the quality of life and the personality structure of a human being and the way in which they are implemented is determined by so-called Odús.
- The Odús or ways and structures are led by 16 Orixás and they correspond to essentially defined phases of life with specific challenges. The understanding of the personal path indicated the individual spiritual map of a human being. The 16 central Odús corrispond to 16 central Orixás.
- In Cuba the Orixás are much more present than the Odús (cf. Plöger 2016: 42 ff.).

16 major Orixás in Cuba
Orixás: are the sum of all qualities existing in the Universe

CUADRO 1.- DEIDADES DEL PANTEÓN LUCUMÍ Y SACRIFICIOS ASOCIADOS

Deidad	Santo católico	Poderes o aché	Sacrificios
Olofin y Olordumare	Idea suprema de Dios	Concede aché	___
Obatalá	Ntra. Sra. De las Mercedes	Dueña de las cabezas	Ratones, palomas, Gallinas de Guinea
Babalú – Aye	San Lázaro	Cura las enfermedades dermatológicas	Tabacos, Palomas, gallinas
Orunbila	San Francisco de Asís	Dueño del artículo	Carnero, paloma, chivo
Changó	Santa Bárbara	Dueño del rayo, los tambores	Carnero, chivo, banana
Ochún	Ntra. Sra. De La Caridad	Dueña del dinero de los cocales y del amor	Chivo, palomas, gallinas
Yemaya	Ntra. Sra. De Regla	Dueña del mar	Carnero, pescado, palomas
Olokun	Ntra. Sra. De Regla	Dueño del mar	Los mismos que Yemaya
Elegua	San Antonio, El Ánima Sola	Dueño de los cuatro esquinas	Gallo, aguardiente con pimienta de grano
Oggún	San Pedro	Dueño de los hierros y el monte	Perros, cocos, jutías
Agalla	San Cristóbal de La Habana	Dueño del río	Pescado, carnero
Oya	Ntra. Sra. De La	Dueño del	Alimentos cocidos, palomas

Deidad	Santo católico	Poderes o aché	Sacrificios
Inlé	Candelaria / San Rafael	cementerio / Dios de la economía agraria	Palomas, tijeras, pescado
Obeyes	San Cosme y San Damián	Dueños de la fortuna	Sangre por excelencia
Ochosi	San Norberto	Rey de los cazadores y dueño de la cárcel	Palomas y gallinas de guineas
Osain	San José	Dueño de todas las yerbas	Jicotea, gallinas

Fuente: Rómulo Lachatañeré (2001). El Sistema Religioso de los Afrocubanos.

4.3   The Odu or categories of Ifá divination and the Ifá literary corpus

The extensive corpus of texts, spiritual principles and mathematical formulas have not been written down, but were – as part of the Oracle of Ifá – and are orally transmitted in form of thousands of verses called ese. Later they were also passed on as mythological stories in form of narrations (itans). The Oracle of Ifá takes access to the 256 Odus functioning as oracle signs. The babalawo can thereby evaluate a system of Odus (oracle signs/volumes). The 16 basic patterns are combined with each other and result in 256 double signs including different aspects that can be analyzed and interpreted via the verses (ese) and myths (itan) assigned to them. So the Odus help to give meaning and clarity to the thousands of verses and myths that form the Ifá literary corpus. Central is the communication with the spiritual world through the Ifá Oracle that is interpreted on the basis of verses and myths.

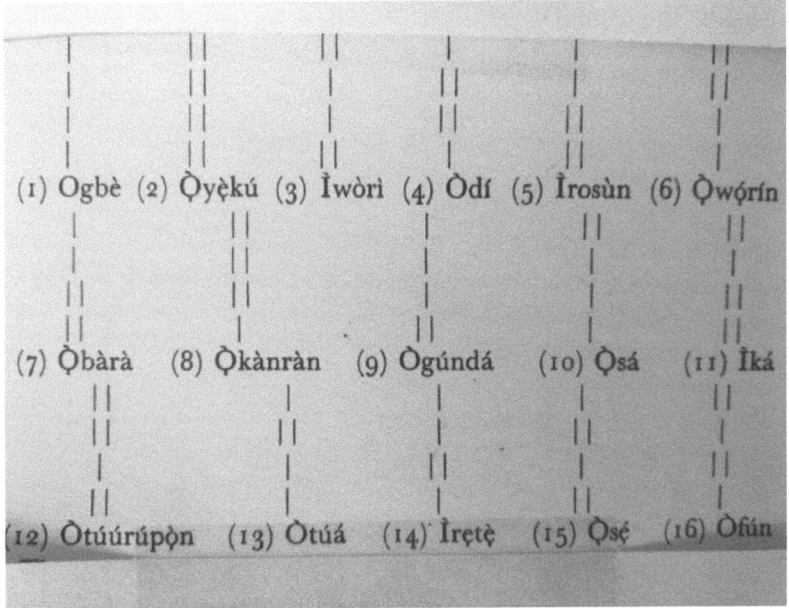

(Source: cf. Abimbola 1977: 16)

The 256 Odu derived from the 16 generic patterns are arranged in two sets. The first and most important set are the Ojú Odù (major Odù). 16 in number and based on a duplication of each of the 16 generic patterns above. Èjì or Méjì (two) = Èjì Ogbè (two Ogbe patterns). The principal 16 Odu are arranged in order of seniority: 1. Èjì Ogbè, 2. Òyèkú Méjì, 3. Ìwòrì Méjì, 4. Òdí Méjì, 5. Ìrosùn Méjì, 6. Òwónrín Méjì, 7. Òbārà Méjì, 8. Òkànràn Méjì, 9. Ògúndá Méjì, 10. Òsá Méjì, 11. Ìká Méjì, 12. Òtúúrúpōn Méjì, 13. Òtúá Méjì, 14. Ìretè Méjì, 15. Òsé Méjì, 16. Òfún Méjì (cf. Abimbola 1977: 16 f.).

Each of the 256 Odu has a distinct character associated with it. E.g. Eji Ogbe, the first Odu, is believed to signify good luck and Irete Meji, the 14th Odu, e.g. related to resurrection. The second Oyeku Meji (see next image) refers to sacrifice and the consequences of neglect of sacrifice:

II Oyèkú Méjì

(a)

Iwo Òyè,
Èmi Òyè;
Òyé ṣẹ̀ṣẹ̀ ńláá bọ̀ lókè.
Wọ́n ṣe bójúmọ́ ní ńmọ́;
A díá fẹja   5
Tíí ṣọmọ wọn lálẹ̀ odò.
Wọ́n ní kẹ́ja ó rúbọ.
Wọ́n ní pípọ̀ nire ọmọọ rẹ̀,
Ṣùgbọ́n kó rúbọ aráyé.
Kò rú.   10
Ó ní báwo làwọn ọ̀tá
Ṣe leè ríran ráwọn ọmọ òun lálẹ̀ odò?
Ó pawo lékèé,
Ó pẸ̀ṣù lólè,
Ó wọ̀run yànyàn bí ẹni tí ò níí kú,   15
Ó kọtí ọ̀gbọin sébọ.
Ńgbà tómọ aráyé dìde,
Wọ́n nawọ́ he okó, àdá àti ọ̀gbùn;
Wọ́n ṣé odò,
Wọ́n si bẹ̀rẹ̀ síí gbọ́n ọn,
Igbà tí omí tán léyìn ẹja àti àwọn ọmọọ rẹ̀ 20
Ni àwọn ọmọ aráyé bá mú wọn,
Wọ́n si fi wọ́n léri iyán,
Àṣẹ Èṣù ni kò jẹ́ kí
Àwọn ọmọ eja ó leè tán láyé.   25
Ṣùgbọ́n títí dòní olóníí,
Àwọn ọmọ aráyé ńkó àwọn ọmọ eja ni.

(b)

Òpá gbóńgbó níí ṣaájú agbọ́ọni;
Atẹ́lẹsẹ̀ méji
Wọn a jìjàdù ọ̀nà gborogàn, gborogàn;
A díá fún ẹrinlójọ aṣọ

II Òyèkú Méjì

(a) The Consequences of Neglect of Sacrifice

You are Òyè[1];
I am also Òyè;
Daylight is just appearing in the skies
But people thought it was already morning.
Ifá divination was performed for Fish
Who was an offspring of the river bed.
Fish was told to perform sacrifice.
They told her that she would have many children,
But she was warned to perform sacrifice to prevent attacks of
    human beings.
She did not perform sacrifice.
She said that it was not possible for enemies.
To see her children at the bottom of the river.
She took her Ifá priests for liars,
She called Èṣù a thief[2]
She looked fearfully to heaven as if she would never die.   [1]
She turned a deaf ear to the warning concerning sacrifice.
When human beings got up,
They took hoe, cutlass and ọgbún.[3]
They dammed the river,
And started to drain off its water.
When there was no water left on top of Fish and her children, 20
Human Beings took them,
And put them on top of pounded yam.[4]
It was the commandment of Èṣù[5]
Which prevented the complete annihilation of all species of   25
    Fish from the earth.

(b) Red Cloth Is Never Used To Cover The Dead

A small walking stick goes in front of he who wades through a
    foot-path on a wet day.[1]
The two soles of the feet,
Struggle persistently for possession of the narrow path.[2]
Ifá divination was performed for one hundred and sixty four
    cloths

(Source: cf. Abimbola 1977: 48 f.)

Most of the ese in each Odu contain stories related to the character or theme of the Odu concerned. Each of the 256 Odu is believed to bear some relationship with one of the divinities. The Odu which is related to a particular divinity is said to be "owned" by or "to belong" to that divinity. Okànràn Méjì contains the myths of Sàngó, while Ogúndá Méjì contains the myths of Ogún. These Odu tell us about the life of these divinities when they were here on earth, their relationship with the other divinities and benevolent powers and their importance to Yoruba traditional culture. "But generally, Ifá divination poetry presents us with a body of myths which depict Yoruba divinities as friends of man (Abimbola 1977: 32)."

Every single Odu has a distinct character associated with it. E.g., Èjì Ogbè, the first and most important Odu, is believed to signify good luck while Ìretè Méjì,the 14th Odu, signifies death. The 13th Odu, Òtúá Méjì, tells mainly the history of Islam and the introduction of that religion into Yorubaland. Each Odu has approximately 800 ese or more. Ifá priests learn to distinguish between the ese belonging to different Odu. The job of the Ifá priest involves the recognition of the signature of each Odu and their interpretation.

Here is an example for an ese Ifá (cf. Abimbola 1977: 21 f.):

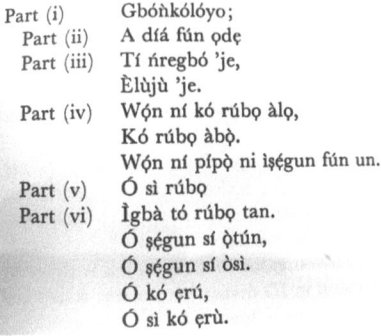

Part (i)   Gbónkólóyo;
Part (ii)   A díá fún ọdẹ
Part (iii) Tí ńregbó 'je,
            Èlùjù 'je.
Part (iv)   Wọ́n ní kó rúbọ àlọ,
            Kó rúbọ àbọ̀.
            Wọ́n ní pípọ̀ ni iṣẹ́gun fún un.
Part (v)   Ó sì rúbọ
Part (vi)   Ìgbà tó rúbọ tan.
            Ó ṣẹ́gun sí ọ̀tún,
            Ó ṣẹ́gun sí òsì.
            Ó kó ẹrú,
            Ó sì kó ẹrù.

Part (vii)   Ó ní bẹ̀ẹ̀ gẹ́gẹ́
            Ni àwọn awo òún ńṣẹnu rereé pe 'Fá.
Part (viii)   Ẹ ṣe ọdẹ ní hiin,
            Hàà hiin.
            Ọdẹ hiin,
            Hàà hiin o.[35]
Part (i)   The Ifá priest named *Gbóṅkólóyo*
Part (ii)   Performed Ifá divination for the Hunter
Part (iii) Who was going to hunt inside seven forests
            And seven wildernesses.
Part (iv)   He was told to perform sacrifice for safety to
            And from the expedition.
Part (v)   And he performed sacrifice.
Part (vi)   After he had performed sacrifice,
            He conquered his enemies on the right,
            He defeated his enemies on the left.
            He captured slaves,
            And gathered a lot of booty.
Part (vii) He said that was exactly
            How his Ifá priest employed his good voice in praise
            of Ifá.
Part (viii) Welcome the hunter with acclamation.
            Welcome the hunter with praise.
            Hunter, we salute you.
            We welcome you with approval.

(Source: cf. Abimbola 1977: 21, f.)

4.4   Ese Ifá

4.4.1   The Structure[29] of Ese Ifá

Abimbola elaborates in detail: "Each Ifá poem has a maximum of eight and a minimum of four structural parts." There are short poems "Ifá kéé kèékéé" and long poems of Ifá "Ifá Ńláálá". "Every ese Ifá begins with a presentation of the names of the Ifá

---

29   Structure as sequential arrangement of elements.

priest(s) who are believed to have performed in the past the divination which forms the subject matter of the poem. (…). The names mentioned in part (i) may not be the names of human beings. They may be the names of animals or plants which are, for the purposes of the story in the Ifá poem concerned, personified so as to be able to narrate a coherent story. (…). Part (ii) of the structure of ese Ifá mentions the name(s) of the client(s) for whom the diviners in (i) performed divination. (…). The third part of ese Ifá (iii) mentions the reason or occasion for the past divination in question. (…). The fourth part (iv) of ese Ifá deals with the motive of past divination and tells us what the client in the past divination was asked to do. This section includes sacrifices. taboos and any other advice the client was asked to observe. (…). Part (v): deals with whether or not the client complied with the advice given to him in (iv) above. (…). Part (vi): tells us the result of the past divination. (…). Part (vii): gives us the reaction of the Ifá priest to the outcome of the divination. (…). Part (viii): is usually presented in the form of a conclusion to the whole story. This section of the Ifá poem may stress the theme of the story or mention the importance of sacrifice. (…). In a culture whose political and social structure is based on divine kingship and the wisdom of the elders, such activities of the past are highly valued and regarded by all (Abimbola 1977: 18 ff.)."

He further elaborates: "All parts of ese Ifá could be chanted or recited by the Ifá priest sharing the process of divination. While chanting or reciting any Ifá poem, the Ifá priest tries to keep as close as possible to the original form of parts (i-iii) and part (viii) as given to him by his own teacher. He is not allowed to add his own words or to sub- stract anything from this part of his repertoire. He is, however, at liberty to use his own language while rendering parts (iv-vii) as long as he keeps in mind the main plot and the characters of the whole story and helps to its original theme (Abimbola 1977: 21)."

4.4.2 Aspects of Style in Ese Ifá

Characteristic features of style found in ese Ifá are repetition, word-play, personification, lexical-matching, metaphor, parallelism and onomatopaea. Types of repetition that can be found in Ifá divination poetry, are (i) structural repetition, (ii) thematic repetition, (iii) linear repetition, (iv) lexical and syllabic repetition, (v) alliteration and assonance (cf. Abimbola 1977: 22 f.).

4.4.3 Content of Ese Ifá

The Yoruba regard ese Ifá as the store-house of their culture. They believe that ese Ifá contain the accumulated wisdom of their ancestors throughout history. So ese Ifá can be defined as a body of historical poems in which the Yoruba culture is preserved. They are in a nutshell:

- the main source of information about Ifá mythology
- Ifá divination poems
- depict the conflict between good and evil – ori – the ajogun and the aje
- relate to the concept of iwa (character)
- emphasize the three things that are supposed to be the most important accomplishments in life (Ire): owo or aje (money), omo (child/children), aiku or alaafia (long life or good health)
- refer to the Yoruba view around them (cf. Abimbola 1977: 41 ff.)

Main source of information about Ifá Mythology, Ifá divination poems

Ese Ifá can be described as a body of historical poems in which the "true" facts of Yoruba culture are preserved. Ese Ifá is especially important as a source of information on Yoruba cultural history and a main source of information about Yoruba mythology (cf. Abimbola 1977: 41 f.). Certain Odù whose ese contain the myths of some Yoruba divinities. Okànràn Méjì contains the myths of Ṣàngó, while Ogúndá Méjì contains the myths of Ogún (32). These Odu tell us about the life of these divinities when they were here on earth, their relationship with the other divinities and benevolent powers and their importance to Yoruba traditional culture. "But generally, Ifá divination poetry presents us with a body of myths which depict Yoruba divinities as friends of man (Abimbola 1977: 42)."

Conflict between good and evil – ori – the ajogun and the aje

Ifá divination poems also tell us about conflict between the divinities and the ajogun, a collective name used to describe the malevolent powers; among these are: Ikú (Death), Arùn (Disease), Ofò (loss), Èpè (Curse)m Ēgbà (Paralysis), Òràn (Trouble), Èwōn (Imprisonment), Ése (Affliction). "Many Ifá poems deal with the inevitable conflict between these two groups of supernatural powers over the interests of human beings (Abimbola 1977: 42)." Another important aspect of the conflict between the "evil" and the "good" supernatural powers is the struggle between the divinities and the àje (the witches), one side of the ajogun in this eternal conflict. One ese Ifá mentions that it was Olodumare himself who gave to the aje their evil powers. Therefore, against the evil machinations of the aje human beings have little protection even from the divinities who themselves are sometimes molested by the witches (cf. Abimbola 1977: 42).

Ebo – Sacrifice

Ese Ifá contains also the Yoruba belief concerning ebo (sacrifice). Almost every ese Ifá contains in part of its structure, exhortations to the clients to perform sacrifice. Performing sacrifice is compulsory to every individual, no matter whether the ori he chose in heaven is good or bad. The divinities will not support anyone who refuses to offer sacrifice. Sacrifice is depicted as a means whereby a man uses material things in exchange for his own life. It is a means whereby man can influence the supernatural powers so that the good powers may cooperate with him and the evil powers will leave him alone in the execution of his plans on earth (cf. Abimbola 1977: 43).

Iwa (character)

In Yoruba belief it is not enough to have good ori and offer sacrifice. In addition to these two concepts which deal with the relationship of man with the divinities, a man must also struggle to improve his relations with his fellow men. So he must improve his iwa from day to day. Without good iwa, a man has achieved nothing: „Iwa Iesin (a good character is the essence of religion.)." Many Ifá poems therefore mention the importance of iwa to human life. Ifá divination poetry states that a person who does not have good iwa while on earth, will be punished in orun after death. The offering of sacrifice does not absolve one from the obligation of showing good iwa to one's fellow men because it is the wish of Olodumare and the ancestors that human beings should uphold the moral values of the society (cf. Abimbola 1977: 43).

4.4.4 The Dramatic Basis of Ese Ifá

In order to be able to appreciate fully the dramatic context of Ifá Oracle in Yorubal-
and, it is important to realize the following key points and thesis statements:

a. Dramatic performances of various forms of beauty and complexity have always
    been an essential ingredient of African cultural life and traditions.

b. Dramatic performances in the African traditional life could be in terms of form,
    ritualistic, religious, secular, mimetic, representational or expressive, according
    to the cultural environment, function and origin of the performance.

c. African dramatic performances are essentially socio-occasional displays

d. They provide a context, a medium for music, dance, drumming, worship and
    literary artistic creativity.

e. African dramatic festivals promote moral education aesthetic and artistic crea-
    tivity and develop people's religious awareness, cultural sensibility and faith in
    the people's social institutions.

f. A fundamental function of festival drama in the African world is the promo-
    tion of the life-continuity of the people, their prosperity, security, fertility and
    safeguard from evil forces (cf. Akporobaro 2012: 457 f.).

4.5   The old Oracle of Ifá in the Opelé System

- Traditionally the old Oracle is „thrown" with ikins (16 sacred palm-nuts) or connected seeds (opelé). Ikins are 16 sacred palm-nuts – the most ancient and most important instrument of Ifá divination. The nuts are taken from a special palm-tree known as òpè Ifá (Ifá palm-tree).
- Myth: Òrúnmìlà replaced himself on earth with the 16 palm-nuts known as ikin. When his children returned to the earth, they started to use the 16 palm-nuts as instruments for divination to find out the wishes of the divinities.
- Characteristics: the traditional version is very complex, interpretation of the throws is done by singing thousands of verses, many hours to perform the Oracle, original language is Yoruba, purely oral system of knowledge sharing/transmission. In its traditional form existent in some parts of Nigeria. Strenghts: very differentiated view of the paths of a person, analyses profoundly paths and principles of the life purpose, defines ways of decision, life structures (cf Plöger 2016: 115 ff.).

4.5.1   The Paraphernalia of Ifá divination[30]

Ikin – Ifá Divination Nuts

The 16 sacred palm-nuts are the most ancient and most important instrument of Ifá divination. The nuts are taken from a special palm-tree known as òpè Ifá (Ifá palm-tree). The Yoruba believe that this type of palm-nut is sacred to Ifá and should not be used for making palm-oil (cf. Abimbola 1977: 4).

Opele Divining Chain

The diviner uses the Opele in order to communicate with the deity of wisdom or knowledge. In the Yoruba tradition the communication is directed towards Orunmila.

---

30   *The process of Ifa divination:* The client enters the house of the Ifa priest, salutes him and expresses a wish to "talk with the divinity". The client whispers his problem to a coin or a cowry shell or to the divining chain or the ibo. It is believed that the wishes of the client's ori (God of predestination who knows what is good for every person) have been communicated to Ifa who will then produce the appropriate answer through the first Odu which the Ifa priest will cast when he manipulates the divining chain. The Ifa priest then picks up the divining chain after offering a few words of salute to Ifa. He urges Ifa to provide the appropriate answer to the client's problem. The priest then utters the iba (permission from authorities) to ile (the earth), Oludumare, and his masters in the art of divination (cf. Abimbola 1977: 9). He throws the divining chain in front of himself and quickly reads and pronounces the name of the Odu whose signature he has seen. The answer to the client's problem will be found in this Odu. The Ifa priest then begins to chant verses from the Odu which he has seen while the client watches and listens. The priest chants as many poems as he knows from that Odu. Until he chants a poem which tells a story containing a problem similar to the client's own problem. At that stage the client stops him and asks for further explanation of that particular poem. The Ifa priest will interpret that particular poem and mention the sacrifice which the client must perform. When the client is completely satisfied with both the poem he picked for himself as well as its interpretation, he proceeds to perform the stipulated sacrifice. The client must make sure that he/she performs the prescribed sacrifice. Sacrifice is central to Ifa divination and to Yoruba religion as a whole (cf. Abimbola 1977: 10 f.).

Ìbò

Instrument for casting lits, a pair of cowry shells tied together to a piece of bone. The belief is that Ifá will speak to the client through the ibo instruments in order to explain the details of a poem which has already been identified as the appropriate poem having direct bearing to his problem. ibo help to interprete an Ifá poem. They act as a means of quick communication between Ifá and the client (cf. Abimbola 1977: 8).

Ìyèròsùn

Divination powder, sacred symbol of Ifá. Whitish/yellowish powder is obtained from the irosun tree. The powder is put inside opon Ifá (the carved wooden tray).

Ìróké

Carved wooden or ivory object, used to invoke Ifá. Ivory or wood, some with a human figure or head. A symbol of the authority, supremacy of the Ifá priest concerned.

Opón Ifá

The divining tray. The Ifá priest prints his marks on a wooden tray when he uses the secret palm-nuts for divination. The belief is that all human beings possess what is known "Ayanmo" (destiny/fate) and are expected to eventually become one in spirit with Olodumare (Olorun, the divine creator and source of all energy). Thought and action of each person in Ayé (the physical realm) interact with all other living things, including the earth itself (cf. Abimbola 1977: 8 ff.).

4.5.2   The mythology of Ifá- the Ifá Creation Myth

The Yoruba belief that Ifá (or Òrúnmìlà) was one of the four-hundred-and-one divinities who came from òrun (heaven) to ayé (earth). Olódùmarè, the High God, charged each one of these divinities with a particular function to be performed on earth. E.g. Ògún was put in charge of all things related to war and hunting as well as the use of iron implements. Òòṣàálá was charged with the responsibility for moulding human beings with clay. Èṣù, the universal policeman and keeper of the àṣẹ, the divine power with which Olódùmarè created the universe and maintained its physical laws. Ifá who knows all the hidden secretes of the universe was put in charge of divination because of his great wisdom which he acquired as a result of his presence by the side of Olódùmarè when the latter created the universe. His praise name in Akéréfinúsogbón, the small one whose mind is full of wisdom.

The 401 divinities (out of which one was "Ifá or Orunmila") descended from heaven (orun) to earth (aye) into the city of Ifè. "At that time there were no creatures of any kind on the earth. The divinities were the first inhabitants of the earth, Ifè was the first place on earth inhabited by human species (Abimbola 1977: 1)." When the divinities arrived on earth, they found that planet completely covered up with water. Before they left òrun, Olódùmarè gave them a basket-full (calabash-full) of sand, a hen with five fingers and a chameleon. Before the divinities landed, they sent the hen down to Ifè with the parcel of sand. The hen scattered the earth and solid earth appeared. The chameleon then walked on it to find out how solid it was. The divinities then descended upon solid earth and pitched their camps in different parts of Ifè. Hen and chameleon became the first creatures to live upon the moulten primordial earth and the divinities were the first beings to live upon solid land (cf. Abimbola 1977: 2).

After the arrival of the divinities, human population developed at Ifè in two different ways. The divinities married among themselves (male & female divinities) and gave birth to a lineage of men who later became the divine rulers of the Yoruba. Olódùmarè with the help of Òòṣàálá created the human beings proper who became the subjects over whom the divinities and their descendants ruled. Out of the descendants of the divinities, the children of Odùduwà became the most important politically and formed the bulk of the ruling dynasty of the most powerful Yoruba kingdoms. Culminating points in the power of these divine rulers achieved in the imperial organization of the old Oyo Empire (cf. Abimbola 1977: 2). At Ifè Òrúnmìlà settled in a place known as Okè Ìgètí. He lived there for many years, first childless, but later he had eight male children. Later he left Ifè for Adó where he spent his remaining life. A saying: "Adó nílé Ifá (Ado is the home of Ifá) (Abimbola 1977: 2)." There are also other creation myths that have been developed by the Yoruba community (cf. Trieber 2019, Fejoo 1986).

5.   New Oracle of Ifá in Cuba

Due to the colonial history, a lot of knowledge got lost, but despite of this traumatic past, the native religion remained the basis for Yorùbá life in Cuba[31]. In Cuba there was a lack of babalawos[32] and people therefore tried to restructure and reorganize what they remembered by themselves. Also this circumstances required the development of a minor divination system for Ifá, namely the awo merindilogun or the 16-cowries divination that already possessed a corpus of stories, but lacked the depth and authority of the traditional Ifá Oracle corpus. "Odu[33] stories provided their foundation for reconstructuring, redefining, and interpreting the new world (Flores-Peña 2016: 212)." Many aspects of the ancient Southwest African Ifá Oracle, the central divination system, were simplified and reduced, e.g. minor oracles developed such as the cowrie shell divination system using sixteen cowries (cf. Flores-Peña 2016: 212). The approach became more pragmatic in nature, focusing stronger on problems of daily life than on comple questions related to meaning and purpose of life as the old

---

31   The Cuban ethnologist Fernando Ortiz wrote many books and essays about the Yoruba and Bantu cultures, among others *entre cubanos, psicología tropical* (1987), *contrapunteo cubano del tabaco y el azúcar* (1991), *los bailes y el teatro de los negros en el folklore de Cuba* (1951).

32   "(...) the lack of babalao as the main reason for this early development of Lucumí practices (...). Old pracices developed without Ifá. Now that the cult of Ifá has been established, many advocate a return to a more 'African practice'. Researchers assume the existence of Ifá as a body of knowledge and the babalao as guardians of such knowledge. However, Lucumí created a new religion out of the parallel recollections of Congo and Yorùbá cults, which were later united by the Ifá epistemology (Flores-Peña 2016: 213)."

33   Odu identifies two aspects of the religious culture: 1. sacred account of events (historical and mythical) that the diviners use to instruct, diagnose, and solve problems; 2. the name refers to the way in which one diviner graphically writes divination figures. In the case of Ifá, the figures are created using lines and circles vertically from left to right. Dilogún, by contrast, uses Arabic numerals. Seen as less influential, dilogún or awo merindinlogun is a divination system that uses sixteen cowrie shells. Each one of the divinities has his or her own set of dilogún (cf. Flores-Peña 2016: 213).

Ifá Oracle did. The system in Cuba is similar to the traditional Ifá, but more limited in the scope of stories it possesses. Ifá is only available to initiated men, whereas the dilogún is accessible to both men and women (cf. Flores-Peña 2016: 213).

Also as the Lucumí community evolved during slavery and after the Cuban republic was founded, it became polarized: "Priests of Ifá, the babalawo, claim a divine right to religious supremacy, based on their close links to Africa and the court of Oyo in Nigeria (Flores-Peña 2016: 212)." According to Miguel Barnet much has been written about the liturgy and theogony of the diverse Cuban religious systems like the Santería or Regla[34] de Ocha and Regla de Palo Monte or the religion of the Congos, less though about the origin of the respective cults and their general terminologies. When the family bonds of the to Cuba displaced Africans broke and their system of relations completely dissolved, the cults had to reorganize themselves and adapt to the Cuban environment and society which led to a very specific process of transculturation related to the worship of specific gods and goddesses, forms and objects of cults and religious beliefs (cf. Barnet 2000: 8).[35] Important in the process of preservation of African traditions, was the founding of religious associations called cabildos[36].

---

34   Regla means „cult"
35   „Die Regla de Ocha oder Santería oder die Regla de Palo Monte sind nichts anderes als das: die Transkulturation von Elementen, die ihre Pflanzstätte in Kuba fanden und die uns mit einem kraftvollen Lebenssaft genährt haben, welcher der kubanischen Kultur eine ganz besondere Würze verleiht (Barnet 2000: 8)."
36   Cabildos were religious associations created to group slaves of similar ethnic origin under the advocacy of a patron saint: "Yorùbá religion was preserved in the urban cabildos, (...) (1993, 73) (Flores-Peña 2016: 213)." Rural cabildos had contact with other ethnic groups that were already in Cuba, e.g. the Cabildo Santa Teresa in Matanzas.

Flores-Peña (2016) focuses on the use of pataкí/patakines by Lucumí diviners (babalawo and oriaté) and emphasizes that diviners transmit religious and cultural knowledge and assert authority through the telling of pataкí that are sacred narratives contained in the Odu corpus. As said this corpus of sacred narratives – sacred poetry and stories belonging to Ifá, the culture's paramount divination system – originated among the Yorùbá of Southwest Nigeria. "But it is in the sacred stories of Ifá that practitioners of Oricha worship find their place in society and learn how to relate to others. It is through pataкí that diviners define matters of power, rank and authority (Flores-Peña 2016: 212)."

Pataкí or myths in Cuban culture can be traced back – more or less completely – to the ones imported by African slaves and are conserved in the religious expressions of the respective ethnic groups. The objective of each mythology is the representation of the origin and history of a group of jointly related gods in form of a pantheon; this is particularly valid for Afro Cuban myths. Nowadays all over Cuba religions are being practiced, whose mythological roots are located in Africa, but have since become acclimatised to their own mythic form. This is especially true for the Abakuá-society as well as for the Arará and Yorubá, whose mythic forms are popularly known as Pataкí. These mostly still orally transmitted myths in form of simple stories could be spread across the island and therefore come to vernacular esteem with also practical and secular use for daily life (cf. Barnet 2000: 9 f.).

Barnet emphasizes that the divination systems used in Afro Cuban religious practices are based upon a polymorphic mythological foundation.[37] The Merindinlogun

---

[37]   „Denn es ist offensichtlich, daß sich alle in den afrokubanischen Religionen benutzten Wahrsagesysteme auf eine vielgestaltige mythische Grundlage stützen (Barnet 2000: 11)."

Oracle majorly uses cowrie shells for divination. The shells are thrown and fall either with the front or the back up. The Oracle can related to 16 basic signs that are similar to the Odu Ifá Oracle signs. Traditionally in Cuba only 12 signs are being analyzed. It is also divined with the Ekuele (cf. Opele in the traditional Ifá system) and coconut pieces. Every sign or formula belonging to one of the divination systems such as the system of throwing cocos (tirada del coco), throwing cowrie shells (tirada de los caracoles, dilogún) or to the system of Ifá panels (tablero de Ifá) presumes one or more stories or patakí offering advice to those seeking advice. In the majority of cases the protagonists are the gods themselves giving advice or providing help, but also natural forces and animals can play an important role. So many Patakí organize human interaction and living together (cf. Barnet 2000: 11 ff.). Patakí and divination systems are based upon a mythological foundation.

5.1   Patakí/Patakines as a direct descendant of the Yoruba Itan

Mythological stories in Cuba are popularly known as patakí/patakines and they are direct descendants of the Yoruba itans. These mostly still orally transmitted myths in form of simple stories could be spread across the island and therefore come to vernacular esteem with also practical and secular use for daily life (cf. Barnet 2000: 9f). Patakí is the main metaphor of the culture ("creation of the world (Ejiogbe)...") and everything is created by the narration of the patakí and its subsequent manifestation in a particular Odu or Oracle. Telling the patakí happens mostly during initiations, opening of the year ceremonies, private consultations and Ifá divination sessions for newly initiated priests. Every sign or formula belonging to one of the divination systems such as the system of throwing cocos, throwing cowrie shells or to the system of Ifá panels presumes one or more stories or patakí offering advice to those seeking advice. In the majority of cases the protagonists are the "gods" (Orixas) themselves giving advice or providing help, but also natural forces and animals can play an important role. So many patakí organize human interaction and living together (cf. Barnet 2000: 11 ff.).

The Merindinlogun Oracle possesses a corpus of stories, but compared to the traditional Ifá corpus they lack depth. Also the new Cuban prose version of ese Ifá does not have the adornments of the traditional ese; it concentrates on the most basic plots. Lineages, places, and characters became condensed and new characters emerged in the Cuban Ifá stories, e.g. that of Mofá[38]: "Lucumí reduced the introductory section to a phrase or refrán that admonishes and sets the tone for the story or patakí, 'la lengua es el azote del cuerpo; el que mucho habla, mucho yerra' ('the tongue is the whip of the body; he who talks a lot, makes a lot of mistakes') (Cortés 1980, 218) (Flores-Peña 2016: 214)."

The patakí in form of simple stories are still orally transmitted and can so be spread across the island. It can be summarized:

- Patakí and divination systems are based upon a mythological foundation
- Patakí is a direct descendant of the Yoruba itan
- Lucumi reduced the introductory section to a phrase or refrain that admonishes and sets the tone for the story or patakí

---

38   Mofá is a contraction of Omo Ifá, the child of Ifá. He appears often in a place of Orúnmila and represents the babalao as a group (cf. Flores-Peña 2016: 214).

Very often – like the itan and ese – patakines provide information :

- about Ifá Mythology and the lifes of the Orixás
- the environment (personification of objects, animals, nature…) – or
- they deal with the conflict between good and evil – or
- with the question what a good character, a good person is.

Here is one Cuban example of a creation myth:

Pwataki Creation Myth

Obatalá, el Cielo, se unió a Odudua, la Tierra, y de esta unión nacieron Aganjú e Iemanjá respectivamente, Tierra y Agua. Iemanjá desposó a su hermano Aganjú, de quien tuvo un hijo, Orungán.

Se apasionó éste por su madre y comenzó a perseguirla, hasta que un día la violentó, aprovechándose de la ausencia paterna.

Iemanjá se puso a correr, perseguida de Orungán, que le proponía vivir con ella. Ya iba a alcanzarla y ponerle las manos sobre ella, cuando Iemanjá cae al suelo de espaldas. Entonces su cuerpo comenzó a dilatarse, a crecer desmesuradamente, hasta que sus senos comenzaron a soltar dos corrientes de agua, que se reúnen hasta formar un gran lago. El vientre se rompe y de él salen los siguientes dioses: 1) Dada, dios de los vegetales; 2) Xangó, dios del trueno; 3) Ogún, dios del hierro y de la guerra, 4) Olokún, dios del mar; 5) Oloxá, dios de los lagos, 6) Oyá, diosa del río Niger; 7) Oxun, diosa del río Oxun; 8) Obá diosa del río Obá; 9) Orixá Okó, dios de la agricultura; 10) Oxússi, dios de los cazadores; 11) Oké, diosa de los ciervos; 12) Ajé Xaluga, dios de la riqueza; 13) Xapanam (Shankpanna) dios de la viruela; 14) Orún, el sol; 15) Oxú, la luna.

(cf. Feijoo 1986: 241)

5.2   Paraphernalia of Ifá Divination in Cuba

The following divination systems are practiced in Cuba today:

La tirada del coco or oráculo Biagué[39]

It is said that one day Olofín came down to the earth and said to the palm coconut tree that it shall not only provide fruit and oil to the human beings, but also it can be used by all the Orixas to foresee the future. So the pieces of the fruit would contain a significance that only the gods would be able to decipher. It is said: "Before Biagué passed away, he had taught the secrets of the divination method to his son Adiatoto (Adoto). His two stepsons tried to betray him and to deprive him of his heritage, but in the end the cocos told the truth and herewith Adiatoto regained what him belonged. He then trained more people how to use the coco as medium of ascertaining the truth. Different positions and patterns are formed by the coco pieces and stand for certain indications and advices; for example if the four coco pieces fall with the white side upturned, the position is called Alafia and the response to the question asked by the consulting person is yes. In case three pieces show the white side and one its black side upturned, the position's name is Otagüe and the Oracle answers whether the related content of the question is possible. Further Eyife describes the position two white and two black cocos face up and refers to a more decisive way of confirmation, saying yes, whereas Okanna Sodde, three black and one white coco face up symbolizes a negative answer (no) and can even announce a

---

39   The eldest divination technique. Biagué was a priest and the first who had used this divination method.

tragedy. A negative position is Oyekun, four black cocos upturned and referring to a no, to death, suffering and tragedy (Efundé 1978: 89 ff.)."

Dilogun or la tirada de los caracoles

The Oracle of caracoles (shells) or the *Dilogun* (as it is called in Cuba) is being used to ask for advice, to heal and to know, to look ahead and to foresee. This Oracle can be consulted by all santeros and santeras. It is composed by 16 caracoles cauris (cowrie shells) that are being thrown on the floor. Since the ritual is quite complex and requires many years of study and learning,

Tratado de Oddūn de Ifá / tablero de Ifá – la vista del tablero por los babalawos

The tablero de Ifá is the divining tray. Like the opón Ifá in the original African tradition, it is used by the priest to leave marks on the tray while doing the divination.

La tirada del opkele y el atepon del babalawo

Similar to the opele divining chain in the original Ifá tradition, the "tirada del opkele" is used as a means to visualize the communication with the spiritual world.

6.   Final observations and assumptions

There is a multitude of research studies that solidify the theory that the current Cuban traditions of patakí and divination systems have developed from the more ancient and older African Ifá Oracle and mythological system.

The Cuban context required a minor divination system for Ifá, called the Merind-inlogun or 16-cowries-divination system. As the ancient Oracle, also the Merind-inlogun possesses a corpus of stories (pataki), but in comparison to the Ifá corpus differs from it in depth and authority. The new Cuban prose version of ese Ifá/itan did not have the same adornments and concentrated on the most basic plots; further more lineages, places, and characters became condensed and stories simplified and new characters developed and replaced others (cf. Flores-Peña 2016).

Further research has to be undertaken regarding the question whether the basic content that had already been expressed in the ancient African ese Ifá/itan remained the same in the Cuban pataki tradition.

References

Abimbola, W. (1977): Ifá *Divination Poetry*, New York, London, Lagos: NOK Publishers Ltd.

Akporobaro (2012): *Introduction to African Oral Literature*, Princeton: Princeton Publishing Company.

Barnet, M. (2000): *Afrokubanische Kulte, Die Regla de Ocha, Die Regla de Palo Monte*, Aus dem Spanischen von Ulrich Kunzmann, Frankfurt a./M.: Suhrkamp. Originalausgabe (1995): *Cultos afrocubanos*, Havanna: Ediciones Unión.

Cabrera, L. (1979): *Reglas de congo, palo monte, mayombe*, p. 15-16, Miami, Florida: Peninsular Printing, Inc.

Delgado Torres, A. E., Agunda La Maza (2005*): El Gran Libro de la Santería, introducción a la cultura yoruba*, Madrid: La Esfera de los Libros.

Díaz, J. C. (2018): *The plants of Santeria and the regla de Palo Monte, uses and properties*, Panama City: Aurelia Ediciones.

Efundé, A. (1978): *Los Secretos de la Santería,* 2nd Edition (1983), Miami: Ediciones Cubamérica.

Evans, L. (2009): "The Black Atlantic: Exploring Gilroy's legacy", *Atlantic Studies , Global Currents*, Volume 6, 2009 – Issue 2, Tracing black America in black British culture.

Fabre, N. ( ): *Main Features of Palo Monte: A hierarchical religion.* New Jersey: Ramapo College.

Feijoo, S. (1986): *Mitología Cubana*, Havanna: Editorial Letras Cubanas.

Flores-Peña, Y. M. (2016): "Mofá and the Oba: Translation of Ifá Epistemology in the Afro-Cuban Dilogún", in: Olupona, Jacob K., Abiodun, Rowland O. (Eds.) (2016): *Ifá Divination, Knowledge, Power and Performance*, Bloomington, Indianapolis: Indiana University Press.

Gómez Nieves, R. (2016): *Patakines and foundation of Ifá*, Havana: Ediciones Cubanas Artex.

Guillén, N. (2005): "Sugarcane", in *Yoruba from Cuba*, Trans. Salvador Ortiz-Carboneres, London: Peepal Tree Pres.

Diverse Authors (2019): *Manual del Santero en Cuba*, 338 pages, purchased in the Casa de la Cultura Yoruba in Havana.

Nieves, R. G. (2016): *Patakines and foundation of Ifá*, Havana: Ediciones Cubanas.

Olufandey, J. C. D. (2018): *The Plants of Santería and the Regla de Palo Monte, Uses and Properties*, Panama City: Aurelia Ediciones.

Ortiz Fernández, F. (1978): *Los bailes y el teatro de los negros en el folclor de Cuba*, Havanna: Editorial Ciencias Sociales.

Ortiz Fernández, F. (1987): *Entre cubanos, psicología tropical*, Havanna: Editorial Ciencias Sociales.

Ortiz Fernández, F. (1991): *Contrapunteo cubano del tabaco y el azúcar*, Havanna: Editorial Ciencias Sociales.

Rauhut, C. (2012): *Santería und Globalisierung in Kuba, Tradition und Innovation in einer afrokubanischen Religion*, Religion in der Gesellschaft, Band 33, Hrsg. von König M., Laube M., Pollack D., Tyrell H., Welgner G., Wohlrab-Sahr M.; Würzburg: Ergon Verlag.

Segal, R. (1995): *The Black Diaspora: Five Centuries of the Black Experience Outside Africa,* , New York: Farrar, Straus and Giroux.

Suárez y Romero, A. (1985): "Canciones de los negros (1853)", *La casa del trapiche, in : Costumbristas cubanas del siglo XIX, selección, cronologia y bibliografia S. Bueno*, Caracas, pp. 325-329.

Tamayo, I. G. (2018): "Las religiones afrocubanas parte indisoluble de la identidad cubana", Revista Caribeña de Ciencias Sociales (mayo 2018). Online: https://www.eumed.net/rev/caribe/2018/05/religiones-afrocubanas.html   //hdl.handle.net/20.500.11763/caribe1805religiones-afrocubanas

Trieber, J. M. (2019): "Creation: An African Yoruba Myth, An Adaptation", online: https://jstor.org, pp. 114-118.

UNESCO intangible world heritage (2008), text & documentary films "The Ifá Divination System (2009)": https://ich.unesco.org/en/RL/ifa-divination-system-00146; Ifa Group of Oyo (2004): "Ifa of the Yoruba People of Nigeria (2004)": http://www. unesco.org/archives/multimedia/document-3742

Wirz, A. (1984): *Sklaverei und kapitalistisches Weltsystem*, Frankfurt a.M.: Suhrkamp.

Zeuske, M. (2003): „Kuba und die „schwarze Karibik". Überlegungen zur unvollendeten Weltgeschichte der Sklaverei", in: *Comparativ 13,* Heft 4, pp. 23-41.

Zeuske, M. (2018): *Sklaverei, Eine Menschheitsgeschichte von der Steinzeit bis heute,* Ditzingen: Reclam.

III

DEATH AND MIGRATION IN THE CUBAN TRADITION OF PALO MONTE MAYOMBE

Abstract

Two dominant Cuban religious groups can be differentiated, namely the Santería or Regla de Ochá, La Regla de Ifá or Lucumí (Yoruba) and Palo Monte Mayombe, colloquially known as Palo Monte or Las Reglas de Congo, La Regla de Mayombe. In short it can be referred to regla lucumí (Western African origin) and regla conga (Central African origin) (cf. Cabrera 1993: 70).[40]

In this paper the focus is on the Cuban tradition of Palo Monte[41] and inherent mythological concepts related to death and migration as well as to healing. Within the Palo Monte tradition the central beliefs circulate around the veneration of spirits and natural/earth powers. Earth/world, nature/wilderness and el monte are the same: "Tierra y monte son lo mismo (Cabrera 1993: 17)." Monte means earth within the concept of universal mother, source and origin of all life. Especially in Palo Monte it is believed that all natural objects (particularly sticks) are infused with powers,

---

40 The word regla can be translated with cult or religion; it refers to rites and religious and magical practices that during the colonial times were imported from African countries and over time also might have been altered or changed or became syncretized with Catholicism.

41 A palo is a segment of wood, often a stick, monte is the forest or a natural area.

whereas the Orixas of the Santería tradition are associated with archetypal human beings.

The ancestral divinities and powerful spirits life in el monte[42], here live the Orixas as well as the dead and the diseased (the Eleko, Ikus, Ibbayes, etc.). The kapok tree as the sacred tree of the Yoruba and Palo religions is the "place" where the dead and the deceased go and stay. The dead – according to the Palo tradition – are believed to live among us – wither in transmigrated form or on non-physical planes of the cosmos. In the religion of Palo, Nzambi a Mpungu – the Congolese name for a high creator god – is the god who created the universe and animates it. Nzambi resides in all natural things and the spirits of the dead.

---

42   «El monte es sagrado' porque en el residen, 'viven', las divinidades. Los santos estan mas en el monte que en cielo (Cabrera 1993: 17)."

El Monte (Wilderness/Earth/Nature)

"We are sons of the Forest[43] because life began there,

The Saints are born in the Forest and

our religion is also born in the Forest.

Everything is the Forest."

"Tierra y monte son lo mismo (Cabrera 1993: 17)."

LYDIA CABRERA

1.   Myth, Religion and Cuban Society

As already mentioned in my presentation and article on the Ifa tradition (La Regla de Ocha Ifa or Santeria) held at the Tartu Conference in 2019, Cuba's religious and mythological culture[44] can be described as a Christian-African Syncretism, the major

---

43   Ceiba is the sacred tree where the dead and the mpungus come to meet (Fhunsu 2016: 352).

44   About myth in general and mythological groups in the African culture groups in specific: First of all I'd like to briefly relate to one definition of myth and mythology as found in the work "Schöpfung und Urzeit des Menschen im Mythus der afrikanischen Völker" by Hermann Baumann (1936). For Baumann myth (Mythus) is the "objectified and lasting worldview of human communities (die objektivierte und dauerhaft gewordene Weltanschauung menschlicher Gemeinschaften)", worldview being the result of "insights of socialized people into the secrets of the world (Einsicht von vergesellschafteten Menschen in die Geheimnisse der Welt)" (cf. Baumann 1936: 2). In so far worldview, since it deals with the subject of communities – peoples, tribes, clans, etc. -, is according to him a phenomenon of cultural sciences as well as of cultural history. Baumann emphasizes that myth becomes worldview only through the artistic moment of dramatic performance of elements of faith, realized by engaging personalities and their actions of the supreme kind, but after human model. These persons are then related to the elements of belief in the world view (cf. Baumann 1936: 2). The final definition of myth according to Baumann is then: "Myth is a vivid account of the worldview of communities (Mythus ist anschauliche Darstellung der Weltanschauung von Gemeinschaften) (Baumann 1936: 2)." In the present work (1936) Baumann carefully, as he himself emphasizes, provides a synthetic representation of mythological material of African cultures. He clustered the mythological groups existing on the African continent as follows:

religious or mythological traditions or spiritual belief systems besides Christianity today being:

- La Regla de Ocha Ifá (Regla Lucumi) or Santería from the Yoruba speaking people (Lucumi is the liturgical language of the Santería): the most significant system in Cuba. Alliance with the Yoruba culture (Nigeria, Benin). The system is composed of the "Regla Ocha", the Orixá cult and the priesthood of Ifá. The "Regla Ocha" and Ifá include complex divination systems, ancestor veneration and different levels of initiation (e.g. el Benbe – fiesta de Santo).

- Palo Monte or Regla de Mayombe (Regla Conga) from the Bantu speaking people: has its origen in the Bantú Pueblos. Its belief system is based on ancestor veneration and on the power of the nkinsis (spirits, or an object that a spirit inhabits). Centre of the cult is around the nganga (a Kikongo language term for herbalist or spiritual healer – in Cuba, the term nganga refers to a certain creation made with

---

1. *"manistic mythology (manistische Mythik)"* – the mythology that is based on an intense belief in the extant series of ancestors. (It is secondary to how these forebears are presented; usually they are perceived and recognized as entities in their entirety).

2. *"animistic mythology (animistische Mythik)"* – the mythology that follows on from a doctrine of doctrines, the belief of a soul that is inherent in all or almost all things, but that is permissive (obsession, trance, sleeping dreams, the division of the shadow and life soul, free spirits of nature, etc.).

3. *"preanimistic mythology (präanimistische Mythik)"* – mythology, which is based on the conceptions of physical body substances and does not refer to a soul independent of the body.

4. *"chthonic mythology (chthonische Mythik)"* – the mythology which faith is based on a personally thought-out or personally conceived earthly being.

5. *"lunar mythology (lunare Mythik)"* – a mythology that implies a belief in personally-conceived beings in the moon or in things associated with the moon.

6. *"solar mythology (solar Mythik)"* – the mythology that builds a belief in personally conceived beings in the sun or in beings associated with the sun.

7. *"Uranic mythology (cölare Mythik)"* – a mythology that reckons with a personally imaginary being in the sky (god of heaven, heavenly man, etc.).

8. "atmospheric mythology (athmosphärische Mythik)" – that mythology that culminates in imaginations of personally imaginary beings in thunderstorms, in the rain, in clouds and fog (cf. Baumann 1936: 4 f.).

an iron cauldron into which several items such as bones and sticks are placed. It also refers to the spirit of the dead that resides there. In Palo, it refers to an iron cauldron used to venerate the mpungo which can be used for magic and divination.). Medical knowledge, healing with herbs and plants.

- La Regla de Arara fromt the Arara Dahomey, a less popular tradition, and Los Ñáñigos o Abakuá: ceremonies around the sacred "tambor Ekue" and the figure of the sacred "fish Tanze". Origins: region of Calabar (today Nigeria) (cf. Tamajo 2018).

Two African religions in Cuba were dominant: the Lucumí and the Congo religion (see Barnet 2000: 84). The Lucumí (la lucumí) were of Western African origin, the Congo (la conga) of Central African origin, yoruba being the language and culture of the Lucumí and bantu the one of the Congos. In consequence two cults or religious orientations manifested in Cuba: the Santería or Regla de Ochá, also called La Regla de Ifá or Lucumí (Yoruba) and Palo Monte or Las Reglas de Congo, also called La Regla de Mayombe – in short the two cults are named regla lucumí and regla conga (cf. Cabrera 1993: 70).

In Cuba, the Yorubá culture enjoys the strongest influence of all originally "immigrant" African cultures, not least because of the practice of their popular religion, called "Regla de Ocha" or "Santería". In this article I'd like to focus on the second mythological tradition mentioned above, namely the Palo Monte or Regla de Mayombe (Regla Conga) from the Bantu speaking people. As Barnet emphasizes, the Congo religion at his time used to be more influential than the Lucumi religion (cf. Barnet 2000: 8).[45]

---

45   „Esteban Montejo beschreibt dies (die synkretistischen Prozesse bei den Kongo-Sekten in Kuba) folgendermaßen: ‚Ich lernte in den Baracken zwei afrikanische Religonen kennen: die Lucumí- und

2.   Origin of Palo Monte Mayombe

Miguel Barnet (2000) wrote about the religions of the Congos, the descendants of the "peoples" of Cuba from the Bantu region, in the Cuban context. He dedicated himself specifically to the "Regla de Palo Monte" and emphasized: "The Regla de Ocha or Santeria and the Regla de Palo Monte are nothing else than that: the transculturation of elements that found their planting place in Cuba and which have nourished us with a powerful vitality that is very special to Cuban culture (Barnet 2000: 8)."

Many of the African people deported to Cuba, originally came from the Congo territory. In the majority of the cases the names were given the additional designation "Congo" to demonstrate the association with the Bantu culture. The Congo basin used to be one of the regions that had been devastated extensively during the time of the slave trade. Still today innumerable names of the tribes of the Congo ethnic groups are remembered. Generic names were: Kimbisa, Briyumba and Mayombe to name three of the most relevant Congo-cults with Bantu origin. Others like the Loango, Ngola, Benguela, Musundi, Kunalungo, Kabinde, Basungo, Bakuba and Bushongo denominate unclear points of origin of practicing believers of the Congo religion or in the "Cabildos[46]" or "Cabildos de nacion" (tribal councils). In Cabildos

---

die Kongoreligion. Die Kongoreligion war bedeutender. In Flor de Sagua war sie sehr verbreitet, (...) (cf. Barnet 2000 84).'"

46   The Congo Cabildos traditionally were associations of slaves who jointly organized festivities and celebrations and also practiced cultural rites (e.g. initiation rites, funeral rites) as well as secret religious rites. Different groups were hereby able to organize themselves separately, so that they could maintain their diverse set of rituals, music styles and other cultural characteristics. During the colonial era there were many "Cabildos congos", primarily in the provinces Las Villas and Matanzas. One of the most famous and popular Cabildos was the one of the Congos Reales (cf. Barnet 2000: 76 f.).

Afro Cuban religious rites and ceremonies for the ancestral spirits – later also in the context of the Ñáñigo[47] cult – could be held (cf. Barnet 2000: 75 ff.).

Until the end of the 18th century the Cabildos faced an intense growth, but only a few decades later during the epoch of the preparation of the first war of independence their existence was completely prohibited. They were accused to be institutions favouring magic and witchcraft which can be seen as a result of a long and systematic discrimination by the Catholic Church.[48] Nevertheless some of them continued to exist; e.g. Barnet refers to so-called "Cabildos congos" of the Musundi and the Loango, of the Kunalungo and the Kunalumbu in Las Villas, Sagua la Grande being the most important Cabildo of the time. Rituals and cults were so able to be preserved in an organized and structured way; some of them were able to exist until the first Worldwar (cf. Barnet 2000: 78 ff.).[49] After the Cabildos had vanished, temple houses remained in which diverse streams of Congo influences became united and

---

47   The ñáñigo is also known as an *íreme* (spirit dancer): http://theappendix.net/issues/2014/4/el-nanigo-spirit-dancer-of-afro-cuba

48   Palo Monte/Regla Conga wurde von kubanischen Ethnologen wie Cabrera und Barnet und anderen oft als "böser Ritus" bezeichnet, vermutlich die Folge einer langjährigen Defamierung und Diskriminierung durch die Katholische Kirche (cf. Barnet 2000: 91). "Regla Conga oder Regla de Palo, Palo Monte: Das ist die umfassendste Vorstellung, die es überhaupt gibt. Sie widerspiegelt die Gegenwart des Palo del Monte ("Waldbaum") als eines Elementes der magischen Beschwörung. Unter diesem Begriff lassen sich auch andere Tendenzen der Congo-Sekten in Kuba zusammenfassen, tatsächlich vereinnahmt sie beinahe alle Zauberriten der Übrigen. Das Mayombe oder Palo Monte gehört zudem an allgemeinsten bekannten und populärsten Riten. Man sagt, daß es Böses bewirke, "jüdisch" und nicht "christlich" sein, daß es dem Unkraut gleiche und mit Toten zu tun habe. Darin praktiziert man "böse Riten", man benutzt Kohle und Schießpulver für die "Arbeiten (Zaubereien)", die man vorzugsweise dienstags durchführt, weil dies "der Tag des Teufels ist" (Barnet 2000: 92)." Ambivalente Sichtweise, für die einen ist der Ritus/die Religion heilsam und konstruktiv, für die anderen einen bösen Zauber praktizierend (cf. Barnet 2000: 96).

49   During the whole colonial period and as well afterwards, as Lydia Cabrera (1979) reported, these "Cabildos congos" and Cabildos of other nations such as the Basongo, Mumbona, Bateke, Mundemba, Bakongo, Musabela, Kabinda, Bayaka, Benguela, Mondongo, Mayombe, Ngola, etc. remained part of Havana and other cities and villages of the island.

hereby unclear and more ambiguous and generally each of the Congo-temples or "Casas de palo" were headed by a priest or father[50]. It was custom that in a praise house of Palo Monte Mayombe a strict hierarchy was/is to be followed.

Hierarchy in Palo Monte Mayombe praise house
(inspired by/cf. Fhunsu 2016: 281)

House of the Nganga
(Casa Mundo a Nso Nganga - a group of believers;
like a tribal organization or an old cabildo of the Kongo)

|

Padre Nganga = Amo
("the master, the authority":
"abiding by the bunganga of the elders"/"putting in practice the knowledge,
the know-how, sacred legacy of the ancestory (Fhunsu 2016: 281)."

|

Mayor Domo & Madrina
(godmother of the nganga, "ngudi nganga")

|

Nkombos/Ngombes, Mbua
(dogs/servants of the nganga that the fumbi mounts & moanas
(belong to the house)

---

50   In the Congo tradition the priest often was called either Padre or Tata Nganga (Padre Nganga).

So the priests followed the knowledge and wisdom that had been transmitted orally from their forefathers and fathers; consequently they formed and developed the temple houses and religious practices according to their personal views and in accordance with the traditions of the families and the clans (cf. Barnet 2000: 81).

The slave trade itself caused a social and religious structural change of the cults with Bantu origin. Barnet emphasizes that the flexibility of these belief systems and their unclear and somehow diffuse past and origin stimulated an imaginative power that was less dogmatic than those of the Yoruba. Fantasy and creativity led to a genesis of syncretistic processes – also elements of Catholicism were incorporated – among the Congo groups in Cuba. The ritual amalgamation and the ethnic heterogeneity of the Cuban Congos is so ample that it is an impossibility to decipher the respective terminologies (cf. Barnet 2000: 88 ff.).[51]

The association of the descendants of each Congo nation became crucial in the preservation of cultural knowledge and identification. Further more it was needed to introduce a common language and – despite of the multiple dialects – to arrive at a standardized terminology, namely the so-called "Bozalŏn"[52] with Congo-origin. Insecurity also existed about the cultural roots of rites, liturgical elements and cults,

---

51   Lydia Cabrera once made an attempt to list the Cuban Congos' original groups; she named the following: "(...): Congo Babundo, Congo Musakamba, Congo Mpangu, Congo Bakongo, Congo Musundi, Congo Loembi, Congo Mbāngala, Congo Kisenga, Congo Biringoyo, Congo Mbaka, Congo Kabinda, Congo Ntōtila, Congo Bangā, Congo Musabele, Congo Mpembā, Congo Makuponko, Congo Kasamba, Congo Motembo, Congo Makuā, Congo Kumba, Congo Ngola, Congo Kisamba, Congo Nisanga, Congo Muluanda, Congo Lundē Butuā, Congo Nbanda, Congo Kisiamo, etc. (Cabrera 1979: 60 f.)."

52   Bozalŏn was the Cuban name for the pidgin the "Negros bozales" (or the in Africa born and to the Americas deported slaves) spoke. The hybrid vocabulary consisted of Castillian words and Congo words stemming from one language family, namely the Bantu (cf. Barnet 2000: 81 f.).

also about gods and half gods and other beings and entities of the Congo-pantheon that can be visualized as follows (cf. Barnet 2000: 81 f.).

Pantheon of the Congo Tradition
(inspired by/cf. Fhunshu 2016: 277 ff.)

Nsambi (The Supreme God)

|

Mpungus = superior spirits (Kimpungulu)

|

water spirits (e.g. Mboma) – comparable to Yemaha/virgin of the … (Mama Kalunga/Pungo Kisimba/Mamma Umba/Mbumba Mamba/Knita Kiamsa/ Four Winds, etc.); see water spirits (nkitas)

and

mountain spirits (e.g. Maninga) – nkita kinseke/minseke …(Mpungo Kiko-rot: Jesus-Christ/Mpungo Lomboan Fula=Ifa/Bakuende Bamba di Ngola=The King Melchior (from the Kongo)/Nsasi=Chango, Saint Barbara, etc.

„(…) the adepts of the Mayombe Rule or Palo Monte Rule recognize above all else, Sambia. For tat reason, it is always said Sambia above, Sambia below, Sambia nsulo, Sambia ntoto. Because there are two Sambias and they are the same Tubisian Sambi Sambia Munansulu: God the Great who is in the sky and Mpungo Sambia bias muna ntoto: Sambia who came to make the world and made everything. But Sambia is in the sky and the Mpungu Nkula, who live under the earth help us as much as the Kafukemba, the people who have already died, fua (Funshu 2016: 279 f.)."

It is very unlikely that elements of the in Cuba surviving Congo-culture can be exactly defined through their ethnographic origin. Rather ritual differences and specific orientations of each Palero – that is the name of a practising devotee of these respective Congo-rules or Reglas de Palo – are determined by ways of syncretism developed in Cuba (cf. Barnet 2000: 81 f.).

What is interesting is that the Congo-religions were easier influenceable than others, since the cults were more animistic and magic in nature and they were based less on a consistent philosophical and mythological fundament than e.g. the Lucumī religions were. Although the Congo-religion was the second cult in Cuba stemming from Africa, it kept a huge impact sphere spread across the entire island before the rise of the Yoruba-religion. The permeability of the Congo sects for other cultic elements had been determined predominantly by the Yoruba influence. Gods, half gods and supernatural powers worshipped by the Congos assimilated elements and traits of the Yoruba gods etc., but still they maintained their own fund of stories based upon an independent Bantu origin. These stories lead into the Congo and its natural environment, to its animals, mountains, rivers and trees. A complete Congo-hagiography can be found – initially it survived in the slave barracks, then in the Cabildos of the colonial era and later on in the temple-houses (Munansos). Certainly can the overwhelming influence the Yoruba had on the Congo-pantheon not be negated, but still the authentic characteristics of the Congo gods have to be acknowledged (cf. Barnet 2000: 83).

3. Nsambi and the supernatural beings of the Congos

Barnet mentions that there is no cult for Sambia or Nsambi/Sambiampungo, no sacrifice or donation of food; the god lives in the abstract (cf. Barnet 2000: 120). "God is transcendent, as the theologians say. He created the world and men. The world bears his mark, his trace. God explains and justifies everything; but he is in the hereafter, high above and unreachable, and the people are down here. The forces of nature are in the forest, in the rivers, in the sea. That universal, inner God and the irrational need to reach him are also present in the Congo groups in Cuba. The Paleros call this god Nsambi or Nzambi, Sambiampungo or simply Sambia. For the Congos, Nsambi is the Supreme Creator, like Olofi in the Santería and like Abasí with the Abakuás (Barnet 2000: 120)."[53]

In more detail the high god is described here: "An important, much discussed high god of West Africa is Nzambi (Nyambi). We translate his name as 'he who forms'; he proves an old creator quality. In fact, Nzambi in West Africa faces the Kalunga in the same way as Kiumbi faces the Mulungu in the East. And in both cases, the Creator God seems to be of a great age. However, the Nzambi name was brought to the most distant areas by Christian influences, so that its wide spread today is relatively recent. But he mostly met gods of the same kind, whose names were also

---

[53] „Gott ist transzendent, wie die Theologen sagen. Er hat die Welt und die Menschen geschaffen. Die Welt trägt sein Zeichen, seine Spur. Gott erklärt und rechtfertigt alles; aber er ist im Jenseits, hoch oben und unerreichbar, und die Menschen sind hier unten. Die Naturkräfte sind im Wald, in den Flüssen, im Meer. Jener universale, innerliche Gott und das irrationale Bedürfnis, ihn zu erreichen, sind auch bei den Congo-Gruppen in Kuba gegenwärtig. Die Paleros nennen diesen Gott *Nsambi* oder *Nzambi*, *Sambiampungo* oder einfach *Sambia*. *Nsambi* ist für die Congos der Höchste Schöpfer, wie Olofi in der Santería und wie Abasí bei den Abakuás (Barnet 2000: 120)."

formed from the same word roots, e.g. Nzakomba, Djakomba, Bumba, Mbomba etc., which express shaping scooping; the Djakomba of the Mongo e.g. similar to Kiumbi in the East, new people take shape (by kneading). Also in the area of the Nzambi high god, who is mostly thought to be enthroned in heaven or far back in the bush, one tells disrespectful stories and human-all-too-human about this god. In places it is – if not often – transformed manistically (something Pangwe and Lunda). The old West African ancient and earth goddess can only be seen in Fiote and Congo mythology, perhaps in the lunar woman of the Sonnennzambi the Rotse, but certainly in the Kamona-Manesse of the Masuko. The position of the savior Libanza in the central Congo, who temporarily merges with the Creator God, is remarkable. What is striking is the importance that the animistic conception of activity spirits, which are connected between God and humans, is gaining in space in the distribution area of the Nzambi Mbumba gods. Here it evidently ties in with related things in Western Sudan, but then also with apparitions in the Zambezi-Nyassa Basin (see Wemba, Tschwana etc.). The development of the Modimo term of the Nkundu corresponds almost completely to that of the Tschwana (cf. Baumann 1936: 28 ff.), And the "belima", "virimu", etc., can be compared with the "milungu", "badimo" and others Spirit beings in the Zambezi Basin can be compared. As an animistic phenomenon, these spirits are to be attributed to the younger African (maternal) plant culture, whose tendency to obsessions and the teachings of spirits often has to occupy us (Baumann 1936: 115)."[54]

---

54   "Ein wichtiger, vielbehandelter Hochgott Westafrikas ist Nzambi (Nyambi). Seinem Namen übersetzen wir mit 'der, welcher formt'; er beweist eine alte Schöpferqualität. Tatsächlich steht Nzambi in Westafrika dem Kalunga in gleicher Weise gegenüber, wie Kiumbi dem Mulungu im Osten. Und in beiden Fällen scheint uns der Schöpfergott ein hohes Alter zu besitzen. Allerdings ist der Nzambi-Name schon früh

So a universally valid etymology for the entire Nzambi area has not yet been undertaken. We can see that reference is made to Dennett, who uses the word "anza",
i.e. "Congo River", "Spirit of the Congo River", "which comes out of the earth",
"nsi ". Nsambi here corresponds to a female earth deity. Others say that the part of
the word "mbi" means "evil and wickedness", "bad world" or "illness" as punishment
for offences against Nzambi (cf. Proyaert 99). There is also a reference to the fact
that Nsambi is good and bad (cf. Baumann 1936: 98 f.).

There is also the mention of Nsambis as "overlord of the universe ('nsa' = earth, sky,
stars, waters, animals, plants, people, ancestors (Baumann 1936: 100)" as well as
"almighty god of heaven (Baumann 1936: 102)". The peoples of the lower Congo call
Nzambi the supreme god, the creator of the world, who withdrew from the world
and people after the creation. The chief god Nzambi ampungu has people made in

durch christliche Einflüsse in entfernteste Gegenden gebracht worden, so daß seine heutige, weite
Ausbreitung relativ rezent ist. Aber er traf meist ganz gleichgeartete Götter an, deren Name ebenfalls mit
denselben Wortwurzeln gebildet wurde, z.B. Nzakomba, Djakomba, Bumba, Mbomba usw., welche ein
formendes Schöpfen ausdrücken; der Djakomba der Mongo z.B. formt ähnlich wie Kiumbi im Osten
dauern neue Menschen (durch Kneten). Auch im Bereich des Nzambi-Hochgottes, der zumeist im
Himmel thronend oder weit hinten im Busch hausend gedacht wird, erzählt man sich despektierkiche
Geschichten und Menschlich-Allzumenschliches von diesem Gott. Stellenweise ist er – wenn auch
nicht oft – manistisch umgeformt (etwas Pangwe und Lunda). Die alte westafrikanische Uralte und
Erdgöttin sieht höchstens noch in der Fiote- und Kongomythologie, vielleicht in der lunaren Frau des
Sonnennzambi der Rotse, sicher aber in der Kamona-Manesse der Masuko heraus. Bemerkenswert
ist die Stellung des Heilbringers Libanza im zentralen Kongo, der zeitweilig mit dem Schöpfergott
verschmilzt. Auffallend ist die Bedeutung, die im Verbreitungsgebiet der Nzambi-Mbumba-Götter
die animistische Vorstellung von Tätigkeitsgeistern, die zwischen Gott und die Menschen geschaltet
werden, an Raum gewinnt. Sie knüpft hier offenbar einmal an verwandte Dinge im Westsudan, dann
aber auch an Erscheinungen im Sambesi-Nyassabecken an (s. Wemba, Tschwana usw.). Die Entwicklung
des Modimo-Begriffes der Nkundu entspricht fast völlig dem der Tschwana (s. Baumann 1936: 28 ff.),
und die "belima", "virimu", usw., können mit den "milungu", "badimo" und anderen Geisterwesen
im Sambesibecken verglichen werden. Diese Geister sind als animistische Erscheinung der jüngeren
afrikanischen (mutterrechtlichen) Pflanzenkultur zuzusprechen, deren Neigung zu Besessenheiten und
Geisterlehren uns oft beschäftigen muß (Baumann 1936: 115)."

pairs by the sub-god Nzambi and Nzambi takes the place of the earth force Bunsi (cf. Baumann 1936: 102).

The Herero have the idea of a high god named "Karunga" or "Ndjambi-Karunga"; Ndjambi is considered the high god and creator of the world, whose name is holy and should therefore not be pronounced (cf. Baumann 1936: 26). The creator god Kiumbe is considered to be the oldest figure of a creator god in the east and also appears as the oldest sky deity of the Pare (Dannholz, 48, p. 13 f.): "It is probably the oldest pure sky deity in East Africa, once from the manistic Mulungu, then again ousted by the solar Izuwa (Zowa) and other gods. Meinhof (Allg. Miss.-Zeitsch. 1923, p. 69 ff.) Derives Kiumba from ku-umba = to scoop (also: in clay forms (Baumann 1936: 62), inserted by the author), which should already be noted that the same root occurs in Nya-mbi, Ndza-kumba, Mdombi and other divine names in the West (...) (Baumann 1936: 44)."[55] He was simply the oldest god in the Bantu area and also arouses here, especially in the West, the minds as Nya-mbi, Nza-kumba, Mbombi, Mbumba (cf. Baumann 1936: 62).

"Dennett explained, as we shall see below (p. 98), Nsambi as both terrestrial and river spirit (Baumann 1936: 80 f.)." At this point it is interesting to mention that in the Bantu countries of Cameroon the belief existed / exists that the subterranean soul realm can be reached through or over water. According to the Soko anthropogony, Zambi prepares people from the river mud; i.e. the transition from the aquatic to

---

55   "Es ist wahrscheinlich die älteste reine Himmelsgottheit Ostafrikas, die einmal vom manistischen Mulungu, dann wieder vom solaren Izuwa (Zowa) und anderen Göttern verdrängt wurde. Meinhof (Allg. Miss.-Zeitsch. 1923, S. 69 ff.) leitet Kiumba von ku-umba = schöpfen (auch: in Lehm formen (Baumann 1936: 62), eingefügt von Autorin) ab, wobei schon jetzt zu bemerken ist, daß dieselbe Wurzel im Nya-mbi, Ndza-kumba, Mdombi und anderen Gottesnamen des Westens auftritt (...) (Baumann 1936: 44)."

the terrestrial element of myth is described here. In most of the Bantu languages the common root word is "longa (river)" or "lunga-longo (clay, earth, land, home)" and refers to the earthly (cf. Baumann 1936: 81).[56]

The Yanzi also know Nyambi, the Tschokwe recognize Zambi as a high god (see p. 85). In the lower and central Congo there is also an earth deity Nsambi in addition to the high god Nsambi Mpungo. In the north-western Congo region we meet the divine name Nyambi (Yambe, Ndyambi, Nzambi, Zambi, Zam, etc.), which means that the name is extremely widespread (cf. Baumann 1936: 94). Nzambi's understanding of the Vili and Fiote of the Loango coast is also interesting. Here Nsambi stands above all. He is the creator of the earth, water, air, plants, animals and people living in heaven and he brings rain, good and bad. So there is the good Nsambi (Ns. A mbote) and the bad Nsambi (Ns. Ambi), but they are usually understood as an ambivalent unit. He is also called Nsambi (a) mpungu, the great Nsambi (cf. Baumann 1936: 99).

Dennett found out that Nzambi-Mpungu was the "almighty god of heaven" among the Fiote, whereby the term "mpungu" meant "the highest" and was different from the godliness "Nzambi". In the lower Congo, too, Nzambi was known as the supreme god and creator of the world, who withdrew from the world and people after the creation. In their stories, the chief god Nzambi ampungu lets the sub-god

---

56 "Dennett erklärte, wie wir unten (S. 98) sehen werden, Nsambi sowohl als Erd-, als auch Flußgeist (Baumann 1936: 80 f.)." An dieser Stelle ist es interessant zu erwähnen, dass in den Bantuländern Kameruns der Glaube bestand/besteht, das unterirdische Seelenreich könne durch bzw. über Wasser erreicht werden (cf. Baumann 1936: 81). Gemäß der Anthropogonie der Soko bereitet Zambi die Menschen aus dem Flußschlamm; d.h. es ist hier der Übergang vom aquatischen zum terrestrischen Element des Mythus beschrieben. In den meisten Bantusprachen ist der verbreitete Wortstamm "longa (Fluß)" bzw. "lunga-longo (Lehm, Erde, Land, Heimat)" und bezieht sich auf das Erdhafte (cf. Baumann 1936: 81).

Nzambi make people in pairs. Here Nzambi takes the place of the earth force Bunsi. Among the Musserongo, a sub-tribe of the Congo, it was reported that Nzambi first created two people, namely Nomandamba and Mandele, with their wives. These then became the ancestors of the blacks and whites. The Nsambi name then spread throughout western equatorial Africa (cf. Baumann 1936: 101 ff.). "Nzambi is in the upper and middle Congo (...) definitely a divine name introduced by the missionaries from the lower Congo (Baumann 1936; 103)."

"The Nzambi of the Lunda on the upper Zambezi comes to earth on a rainbow to create all the animals and plants and the first pair (Baumann 1936: 106)." He lives in Litooma, in the upper, invisible and inaccessible world. In the Bantu area, the composition of the name is explained as follows: Nyambi = Nya + Mbi, "umba" means scoop, create, form, and "Mbumba", the god who forms and creates from clay. Nyambi is therefore the one who creates creatively (cf. Baumann 1936: 107 ff.). Nsambia is different from the concept of god represented by the monotheistic religions. Nsambia is always present in everything of the world, not above them; everything is produced under and within Nsambia in the physical world. After Nsambi followers of the Regla de Palo worship the souls of the ancestors – which is the most important – and of the nature spirits residing in trees, rivers and seas. These powers and beings have their own names and show their specific variants, depending as always on the respective regions of the country or tendencies of the particular cult.

Defining an adequate hierarchy of the supernatural beings or Mpungus is not possible; also they carry an infinite number of names. However the most important beings of the Congo-culture after the Creator god Nsambi are the following:

- Tiembla Tierra – the one shaking the world – is master of the world, the Universe and the four cardinal points and executes all of Nsambi's intentions. He is his advocate and supporter, comparable with Obbatalá of the Lucumí and the Mother of God of the Catholic Pantheon. The Mayomberos know him also as Mama Kengue, an androgynous and omnipotent god.
- Lucero Mundo – evening star of the world – also Khuyu, the Anima Sola of the purgatory or the Infant Jesus of Atocha. He opens and closes paths and is the master of crossroads. He is Elegguá in the Santería or the custodian of the moon for the Mayomberos.
- Sarabanda or Salabanda – he is the god of iron machines and instruments like Oggún in the Santería and Saint Petrus un the Catholic belief. Some Congos equate him with the archangel Saint Michael. Sarabanda is said to be one of the most powerful beings of the Mayombero-cults.
- Siete Rayos – one of the most important gods of the Regla de Palo – Changó in the Santería and the Catholic Santa Barbara, Munalungo for the Mayomberos. He works with fire and gunpowder and is a warrior who helps during difficult and fast magic works. He is also known as Nkita among the Kimbiseros and Mayombe.
- Madre de Agua – Mother of Waters – Siete Sayas (seven skirts), Balaunde; this being is identified with the Holy Virgin of Regla. She is the mistress of the seas and river mouths, Yemayá in the Santería. In all Congo-groups she is highly esteemed and present as nearly no other supernatural power on the landscape of Cuban hagiography.

These are just some examples of Palo Monte supernatural beings, of course there are many other Mpungus belonging to the Cuban pantheon. It can be said that the animistic origin of these cults reminds of the possibility that these spiritual customs went along with totemism (e.g. Bantu totemism) (cf. Barnet 2000: 121 ff).

4.   The philosophical system of Congo rites

Walterio Carbonell: For the Mayomberos "(...) the world is ruled by a substance or a world spirit. The world spirit has the ability to embody itself, that is, to take the form of an ornament, a plant, a stone or even a person. Things take their shape through the invigorating breath of Nsambi (...).[57] Animals, like humans, have an electrical charge. Some animals have greater potential than others, such as the bull, billy goat, maja snake and rooster. The bull feeds the nganga of the Paleros." (Carbonell, Walterio, "Mayombe" en Cuba, Havana, December 1967) (Barnet 2000: 96)."

About the sun, Olorun in Santeria, he says: "The sun is the main source of energy in the universe. The Paleros call them Ntango. A mambo or song to the sun reminds us how important this star is for understanding the existential world (Barnet 2000: 96)." The Mayombero/Palero works with earth, branches, stones, animals, plants, etc. All natural forces, all living – animated and even personified – natural elements can be found in the Congo rites.[58] The Palero uses nature in an openly animistic

---

57 „Sambi, Insambi, Sambiapunguele, Pungun Sambia oder Sambia Mpungu ist der Schöpfer, wie Olodumare, Olorun und Olofie für die Lucumi" (Cabrera, Lydia, Reglas de congo, S. 124) (Barnet 2000: 96)."

58 Über die Sonne, Olorun in der Santeria, sagt er: "Die Sonne ist die hauptsächliche Energiequelle des Universums. Die Paleros nennen sie Ntango. Ein Mambo oder Lied an die Sonne erinnert uns daran, wie wichtig dieses Gestirn für das Verständnis der existentiellen Welt ist (Barnet 2000: 96)." Der Mayombero/Palero arbeitet mit Erde, Ästen, Steinen, Tieren, Pflanzen, etc. Alle Naturkräfte, alle

attitude to explain life. His oracle invokes the gods and forces of nature to express his thoughts[59] (cf. Barnet 2000: 97).

Essential Congo rites of Cuba are the following:

1. Mayombe rite / rule (Regla Mayombe): one can do good and heal (also Christian); free from evil.

2. Regla Briyumba: a popular rite aimed at doing good; has been experiencing an upturn for many years, often in the west of the island in the provinces of Havana and Matanzas.

3. Regla Kimbisa: example of religious syncretism; an older rule / rite. It contains elements of occidental culture, spiritism and Catholicism. Kimbisa is a fusion of superstitious Spanish ideas and popular Catholicism with elements of African rites. Andre Petit, a religious figure of the colonial era, is considered to be the founder of this "rule / religion / rite" (cf. Barnet 2000: 97 f.).

5.   The Nganga and the Performative Arts

A nganga is the dead person (cf. Fhunsu 2016: 329) and as already emphasized "(...); all in Mayombe has to do with the dead, (...) (Fhunsu 2016: 333)."

---

lebendigen – beseelten und sogar personifizierten – Naturelemente sind in den Congo-Riten anzutreffen (cf. Barnet 2000: 97).

59 Oracle systems in Palo Monte/Palo Mayombe are manifold. For example there is the Kongo oracle referring to the shell of the Bafumba, called the vititi mensu. The shells are named bonantoto. By interrogating the nganga, the shells are used to provide the answers "yes" or "no" to questions. The mayombero obtains answers from the spirit.

The Nganga therefore is the fundament of Congo religion and its true centre and focal point. Due to the African elements it contains and due to its age, the Nganga is said to be very powerful and unique.[60] So "Regla Conga" or "Regla de Palo, Palo Monte (the forest tree)" is the most complex representation of Congo belief systems. The Palo del Monte is represented as one element of magic evocation; also other tendencies of Congo sects in Cuba are covered by this term. Naturally Mayombe[61] or Palo Monte belong to the most popular rites (cf. Barnet 2000: 91 f.).

The Congo liturgy is highly complex. The center of this liturgy, its essential focal point, is the nganga. All powers are concentrated in the Nganga, it is saturated with animistic magic, it is earth-rooted magic power. Everything in the nganga has a concentrated power that depends on how long this power has resided in the nganga as part of its message. These Ngangas have evil and good spirits, just like the sacred stones of Lucumi. Without the Nganga there is no Regla de Palo, no Mayombe, without them "there is nothing". All Mpungus, the saints and supernatural beings, are in her. As in a microcosm, all supernatural powers condense in the Nganga. It marks every Tata and every believer; it is a higher prenda, the highest, because the

---

60   "(…); jeder richtet sich nach dem Vorbild seiner Großväter, der Tata Ngangas, und kritisiert die Tendenz des jeweils anderen, (…). Beinahe alle schreiben ihrer Nganga einzigartige Werte zu, wegen der Macht, die isch in ihre verine, wegen der afrikanischen Elemente, die sie aufgenommen habe, oder weil sie so alt sei. Und gerade die Nganga ist die Grundlage der Congo-Religion, ihr wirklicher Mittel- und Brennpunkt (Barnet 2000. 91)."

61   The philosophical system of the Mayomberos is based on the belief that the world is ruled by a substance or Weltgeist (world spirit) having the capability to incarnate itself in form of an animal, a plant, a stone or a human being. The objects or beings adopt their forms through the lifespending breath of Nsambi. "Sambi, Insambi, Sambiapunguele, Pungūn Sambia oder Sambia Mpūngu is the Creator for the Mayomberos as Olodumare, Olorun and Olofi for the Lucumī (Cabrera 1979: 124)" (cf. Barnet 2000: 96).

prendas can be talismans or amulets and can be found in every object or part of such a thing or in trees, stones, shells, bottle gourds, horns, etc. (cf. Barnet 2000: 114 ff.). It also happens that a dancer becomes frenzied, "possessed". When the Congo receives the spirit of a supernatural being in its body and becomes a perro de prenda ("dog of a (magic) pledge", i.e. medium of a nganga). The whole body is "mounted by the spirit of the dead" (cf. Fhunsu 2016: 320-350). The initiate has passed from life to death and then from death has returned to life (cf. Fhunsu 2016: 330). The power of the dead affects him with all its might. Indeed, when we are in the presence of an obsessed Congo who says it was climbed by Madre de Agua (the water mother) or Sarabanda, we often see the pantomime of Yemaya or Oggun, their counterparts among the Lucumi, for the Congo has few Retains mythological elements that could enable him to reproduce the peculiarities of his supernatural beings (cf. Barnet 2000: 111 f.).

6. Congo Dances: Mani und Yuka

Music, dance, and physical expression are instrumental in the process. The dances mani and yuka, which were originally practiced in the slave barracks, are still popular in Cuba. In every Palo house, e.g. at Briyumberos or Kimbiseros, they are listed: for a good effect of the Prenda[62] or Nganga. The dances are emphatically communal; some are couple dances (Palo, Yuka), others (Makuta, Garabato) have an anarchic

---

62 „Pfand": spanische Bezeichnung für Nganga im Sinne von: Grundlage, Zauberkraft, Fetisch, Gegenstand (z.B. ein Topf oder eine Schale), in dem eine übermenschliche Kraft, eine Totenseele haust (vgl. Barnet 2000: 100).

form. However, all of them are associated with a very expressive pantomime (cf. Barnet 2000: 101).

In the dance Mani, men usually dance alone. The Makuta, an old, secret religious dance, was performed in Munanso Bela, the sacred room. The Palo is determined by jerky arm movements; Yuka is a fertility dance. The Congo drums are divided into three groups: 1. the Ngoma, which are very similar to the Tumbadoras (Afro-Cuban vascular drums); 2. the Yuka (Caja, Mula, Cachinko) and 3. the Makuta, which are accompanied by a hoe or an iron stick used as a percussion instrument (cf. Barnet 2000: 102 ff.). The yuka is accompanied by rhythms. As with other groups of African origin, the songs are alternating – soloist and choir alternate, the soloist is called Gallo ("Hahn") and the chorus Vasallos ("Vasallen"). The dances show characteristics that are common to all African dances: one forms rows or circles (…) (Barnet 2000: 110 f.).

The magic name characters ("firmas") also still play an important role. A magical and dynamic element, i.e. the supernatural powers have a number of name symbols, but priests also use them for liturgical purposes. The name signs of the Madre Agua belong to that extensive repertoire of the lingua sacra, which the Africans brought to Cuba in order to express their ideas and beliefs (cf. Barnet 2000: 112 ff.). The Prendas are subordinate forces to the Nganga, and many small groups of believers follow them. For the ritual, the Congos use the Mpake or Mpaka menso, a horn, the inside of which contains some ingredients with magical powers. Brandy, tobacco and even gunpowder are used in these regla de palo rites. The rite is very important to the Congos. The aim is to organize life quickly and successfully with the help of these cults (cf. Barnet 2000: 118).

7.   Concluding thoughts

Certainly the field of healing represents one of the central aspects of the Regla de Palo Monte tradition. Herbs and plants representing the "energy and the spirit where all forces originate (Díaz 2018: introduction)" play an important role in the practice of the same. And thus humility and awe before nature, inherent in this tradition, reminds us of a deep respect for nature and our human nature – an awareness that is necessary to be able to act with our higher consciousness.

Therefore this book ends with a sentence by Lydia Cabrera.

"We are sons of the Forest because life began there,

The Saints are born in the Forest and our religion is also born in the Forest.

Everything is the Forest." (Lydia Cabrera)

References

Barnet, M. (2000): *Afrokubanische Kulte, Die Regla de Ocha, Die Regla de Palo Monte*, Aus dem Spanischen von Ulrich Kunzmann, Frankfurt a./M.: Suhrkamp. Originalausgabe (1995): Cultos afrocubanos, Havanna: Ediciones Unión.

Baumann, H. (1936): *Schöpfung und Urzeit des Menschen im Mythus der afrikanischen Völker*, Berlin: Verlag von Dietrich Reimer / Andrews & Steiner.

Cabrera, L. (1979): *Reglas de congo, palo monte, mayombe*, Miami: Peninsular Printing, Inc.

Cabrera, L. (1989): *El Monte*, La Habana: Editorial Letras Cubanas.

Díaz, J. C. (2018): *The Plants of Santeria and the Regla de Palo Monte, Uses and Properties*, Panama City: Aurelia Ediciones.

Feijoo, S. (1986): *Mitología Cubana*, Havanna: Editorial Letras Cubanas.

Fhunsu, D. (2016): *The Kongo Rule: The Palo Monte Mayombe Wisdom Society (Reglas de Congo: Palo Monte Mayombe), A Book by Lydia Cabrera, An English translation from the Spanish*, dissertation submitted to the faculty of the University of North Carolina, Chapel Hill.

Ortiz Fernández, F. (1978): *Los bailes y el teatro de los negros en el folclor de Cuba*, Havanna: Editorial Ciencias Sociales.

Ortiz Fernández, F. (1987): *Entre cubanos, psicología tropical*, Havanna: Editorial Ciencias Sociales.

Ortiz Fernández, F. (1991): *Contrapunteo cubano del tabaco y el azúcar*, Havanna: Editorial Ciencias Sociales.